HARRISON CANDELARIA FLETCHER

DESCANSO FOR MY FATHER

Fragments of a Life

University of Nebraska Press | Lincoln and London

© 2012 by the Board of Regents of the University
of Nebraska. Unless otherwise noted, all illustrations
are courtesy of the Fletcher family. "Downtown
Albuquerque" postcard photograph by Bob Petley.
Trading card photograph of "Mazambula El Brujo"
(Francisco "Pancho" Salinas) found on *El Mundo
del Ring, Box y Lucha*, http://www.boxylucha.com.
All rights reserved. Manufactured in the United States
of America. ∞

Library of Congress Cataloging-in-Publication Data
Fletcher, Harrison Candelaria, 1962–
Descanso for my father: fragments of a life / Harrison
Candelaria Fletcher.
p. cm. — (American lives)
ISBN 978-0-8032-3839-8 (pbk.: alk. paper)
1. Fletcher, Harrison Candelaria, 1962– 2. Mexican
Americans—New Mexico—Biography. 3. Authors,
American—21st century—Biography. 4. Fathers and
sons—Biography. I. Title.
PS3606.L4767D47 2012   814'6—dc22
2011031847

Set in Galliard by Kim Essman.
Designed by A. Shahan.

For my mother,
and in memory
of my father,
with love

*Absence is the
        highest form
of presence*
JAMES JOYCE

CONTENTS

ACKNOWLEDGMENTS

A number of the essays in this book, often in different forms, previously appeared in the following publications. Many thanks to the editors, judges, and staff who supported my work.

"White," *Fourth Genre* 8, no. 1 (Spring 2006).

"Beautiful City of Tirzah," *New Letters* 72, no. 2 (Fall 2006), was the 2005 recipient of the *New Letters* Dorothy Cappon Churchill Essay Award, a 2007 National Magazine Award finalist, and received a 2008 Pushcart Prize Special Citation.

"Undercurrent," *upstreet* 2 (Fall 2006), was a 2006 Pushcart Prize nominee and a 2006 *Iowa Review* Award finalist.

"Among the Broken Angels," *Puerto del Sol* 42 (Spring/Summer 2007), was a 2006 *Iowa Review* Award finalist and a 2007 *New Millennium Writings* Award honorable mention.

"One Prayer," *Pilgrimage* 32, no. 2 (Fall 2007).

"Hardwood," *Cimarron Review* no. 163 (Spring 2008).

"Inheritance," *New Ohio Review* no. 5 (Spring 2009).

"Rings," *The Dos Passos Review* 6, no. 1 (Spring 2009).

"Relics," *Palabra* no. 5 (2009), was a 2009 Pushcart Prize nominee.

"Wreath," "Brotherhood," "Ash," *Water~Stone Review* 12 (Fall 2009). "Wreath" was a 2009 Pushcart Prize nominee.

"Monster," "Windows," "Stray," *Grasslands Review* 28 (2009).
"Imprint," "Trade-In," "Frames," *Cream City Review* 34, no. 1 (Spring 2010).
"Tremor" and "Pawn," *South Loop Review: Creative Nonfiction + Art* no. 13 (Fall 2011).

"Beautiful City of Tirzah" also appears in the *Touchstone Anthology of Contemporary Creative Nonfiction* (Simon & Schuster, 2007) and *Fearless Confessions: A Writer's Guide to Memoir* (University of Georgia Press, 2009). "One Prayer" also appears in *Telling It Real: The Best of Pilgrimage* (Crestone, 2009). "White" also appears in the *Open Windows III* anthology (Ghost Road Press, 2006).

I would like to the thank the following people for their generosity, advice, support, and friendship: Sue William Silverman, Marc J. Sheehan, Robin Hemley, Judith Kitchen, Philip Graham, Lawrence Sutin, Nance Van Winckel, Phyllis Barber, Mary Domenico, Matt Hudson, Karen Michelle Otero, Barb Page, and Dan Conaway. Thanks also to Kristen Elias Rowley, Sabrina Stellrecht, Jonathan Lawrence, and the wonderful team at the University of Nebraska Press. Most of all, I would like to thank my beautiful wife and children.

DESCANSO FOR MY FATHER

PROLOGUE
Across the Median

I watch my son as thunderclouds gather outside my Denver home. He stomps his wide little feet on the hardwood floor, clamoring for a tube of eucalyptus lotion he cannot reach and cannot have. He balls his dimpled fists into hammers, tugs at the reddish wisps of hair curling around his head like flames. He is twenty-three months old, the same age I was when my father died. I look at him now and try to imagine the impressions he is forming from this time, the feelings he is filing away to retrieve later and hold to the light.

Mood shifting, he gallops away, squealing with delight into the kitchen following a bouncing red ball. And I wonder: if I died at this moment, would he remember me?

❋

Nine years old. Rumbling down a two-lane highway on the way home from a Jemez Mountain stream, cutoffs damp, comics wrinkled, sun slanting through the side window of my mother's '67 Comet. I'm trying to sleep but I'm kept awake by the jolt of potholes and the root-beer breath of my little sister, who snores on the backseat beside me. Hills the color of red chile powder slide by on the horizon, lulling me into a dream. I open my eyes to another bump and it is there—a "t" on the mesa, a cross etched black against the white August sky.

"Someone died there," my mother says, glancing in the

rearview. "Struck by lightning, probably. That's what they did in the olden days. Put up crosses. Little piles of stones."

I sit upright. "Someone's buried there?"

"Oh, no," she says, laughing. "They're memorials. Shrines. It's a Spanish tradition."

She lifts a hand from the wheel and crosses herself.

Our car rounds a corner and the wooden marker fades into the granite and scrub. I close my eyes but the image remains, the person who died without warning, the spirit wandering the roadside like a hitchhiker, watching cars pass, waiting for someone to notice. I see a man, always a man.

❈

For most of my life, my father has been this to me: a silver-haired snapshot, a tarnished ashtray, a broken sword, and a jumble of anecdotes doled out by my mother to the five of us children. When he died of lung cancer on a gray afternoon in August 1964, he left little more than fingerprints, a scattering of artifacts, and silence. My shell-shocked mother, following the advice of a child psychologist, gradually erased his presence from our Albuquerque home. She packed his things in cardboard boxes, placed them inside a hallway closet, and closed the door.

She never remarried, never dated as far as I knew, never mentioned a desire to do so. My father, I assumed, was the love of her life. She was twenty-two when they met, the third of nine children from a Hispanic farming village on the Rio Grande, living a block away from his Route 66 drugstore. He was twenty-nine years her senior, as old as her own father, and twice married, but it didn't matter. He was as kind, witty, successful, and sophisticated as the leading men in the movies of the day, Jimmy Stewart in *Rear Window*, or Cary Grant in *To Catch a Thief*. She defied her parents to marry him. They shared gourmet meals, hosted parties, drove a Cadillac, flew airplanes, and had one child after another. Then he died.

Strip the house of him and he remained, the presence we felt but never spoke of, the crater in our home we pretended not to see.

Since he was the last in his family line, there was seldom mention of relatives. Since I had no tangible sense of him, there was little to miss. The one time I remember kneeling before his white marble headstone in the National Cemetery in Santa Fe, I didn't know what to feel.

And yet, at times, I played in the hallway closet where we kept his things. I zipped and unzipped his orange flight jumper, turned the pages of his musty pharmaceutical journals, and slipped on the cold plastic headset of his broken ham radio set. Then I sat alone in the dark, listening.

❋

Within five years of the funeral, my mother transformed herself. The bookish housewife who baked peanut butter cookies after school had become an artist who protested against the Vietnam War and pinned "Nixon No!" buttons to our grammar school lapels. On weekends she explored the back roads and secondhand shops of New Mexico seeking treasures others had overlooked. Skeleton keys. Cowbells. Crucifixes. Strands of rusty barbed wire. She'd wipe away the dust and cobwebs, load them into the trunk of our peacock green Comet, and nail them to our living room walls. She found comfort and inspiration in these relics, and with them, transformed our house into a museum, cathedral, graveyard, and self-portrait.

I'd often stand beside her while she tied back her chestnut hair with a blue bandanna, placed *The White Album* on the stereo, and assembled her discoveries into "little shrines." After an hour, she'd notice me watching, pull me aside, and point to an antique poker table holding a Pueblo rattle, a vase of dried range grass, a string of Tibetan prayer beads, and a wind-up clock turning in slow dry ticks.

"Look closely," she'd say. "Everything tells a story."

❋

For the portrait of her grandmother, my mother cleared the dining room table of fruit bowls and house cats and spread a wide sheet of manta fabric. With sewing chalk and charcoal pencil she sketched the profile of the old woman seated in a rocking chair wearing a black dress of mourning, her hands in her lap and her head lowered in reflection. With a long, curved colcha needle, my mother pulled strands of yarn through the coarse fabric until her abuela's wrinkled face, iron gray bun, and arthritic hands took shape. Then she sewed a black satin quilt spilling from the figure's lap outside the frame of the wall-sized tapestry. In the fabric, she stitched wedding bands, skeleton keys, rosary beads, picture frames.

For her gallery installation, my mother selected a dozen saucer-sized stones we'd dug from an Algodones arroyo to make a wishing well. With adhesive gel and photo transfers, she affixed the images of dead loved ones to the surface—her grandmother, her aunt Molly, her younger sister Ernestina, my father. She then arranged the stones in an oval pile, face up, framed by the rails of a rusty iron bed.

For her self-portrait, my mother began with a four-panel window she'd found in an adobe ruin near Cochiti. In the upper left panel, she placed a black-and-white photo of her grandmother wearing a black dress. In the second panel, she placed a mirror streaked with sepia ink. In the third, she placed a blank postcard bearing the stamp of her birth year, 1935. In the fourth panel, she placed a bouquet of dried red roses. Lastly, she draped the frame in a black lace veil.

"Can you see it?" she asked me. "Can you see what I'm saying?"

❋

I painted my father. Inspired by my mother's work, I chose a black-and-white portrait she had given me one Christmas—a formal, eight-by-ten, head-and-shoulders shot taken when my father was in his late twenties or early thirties, with thick black hair and Perry Mason eyes. I thought the straightforward pose, perhaps a passport or résumé photo, would be easy to render. I mixed the India ink and gesso and sketched his features as clinically as I would a fruit bowl, studying every contour of his chin, lips, nose, and ears—my chin, lips, nose, and ears. For an hour I looked directly into my father's face, more directly than I ever had. What I saw troubled me. I didn't know who he was. And I didn't know why.

After a week, the portrait remained unfinished, so I did what I'd always done—put it in a closet and close the door.

❀

After college, drawn to the role of observer, I became a newspaper reporter. While driving on assignment through northern New Mexico along the routes of childhood excursions with my mother, I saw roadside crosses wired to guardrails, planted in alfalfa fields, nailed to telephone poles, leaning from cliffs. Some were made of wood. Others iron. Many changed with the season. On Easter they stood adorned with pink and yellow tulips. On Thanksgiving, autumn wreaths. Nearly all included offerings of some kind: snapshots, promise rings, dried carnations, teddy bears, Christmas bulbs, Coors cans.

One August afternoon while researching "Dead Man's Curve," I knelt among the gravel and broken glass of the hairpin turn near Española. Gazing down at the artifacts, I began to assemble portraits. From the portraits, narratives. From narratives, lives. The Vietnam vet who rode a Harley and drank Jack. The high school senior named Rose who collected beanie babies. The farmer who smoked Camels and ate jerky.

In the offerings, I began to see not only the people who had died but the people who had been left behind. In the roadside memorials, I saw two souls trapped in their respective purgatories, the dead and the living, reaching for each other across the median.

❀

Descansos, historians told me. My mother was right. The memorials were called descansos, the Spanish word for resting place. Some scholars believed the practice originated in ancient Rome, where soldiers commemorated the ground of fallen comrades with swords and flags. Others believed descansos came to the New World with Catholicism, spreading to the southwestern United States with the conquistadores and missionaries, who marked with flowers and crucifixes the ground where pallbearers rested en route to the camposantos.

However they originated, historians agreed: a descanso marks the ground of an interrupted journey, the spot where a man, woman, or child died unexpectedly, the point at which a spirit left its body. A descanso reminds us to pray for a soul in purgatory. It is a manifestation of unexpressed grief, a communication, a eulogy, an apology. A descanso is love.

※

Here I sit at my basement desk in Denver, four decades after my father's funeral, surrounded by barbed wire, roots, dried leaves, candles, and rusty nails—the materials of a shrine. In middle age, a father, few things frighten me more than the notion of being forgotten or remaining a mystery to my son and daughter. It is my hope with this collection to write a descanso for the father I never knew, each essay an offering on the path to find him, to find myself.

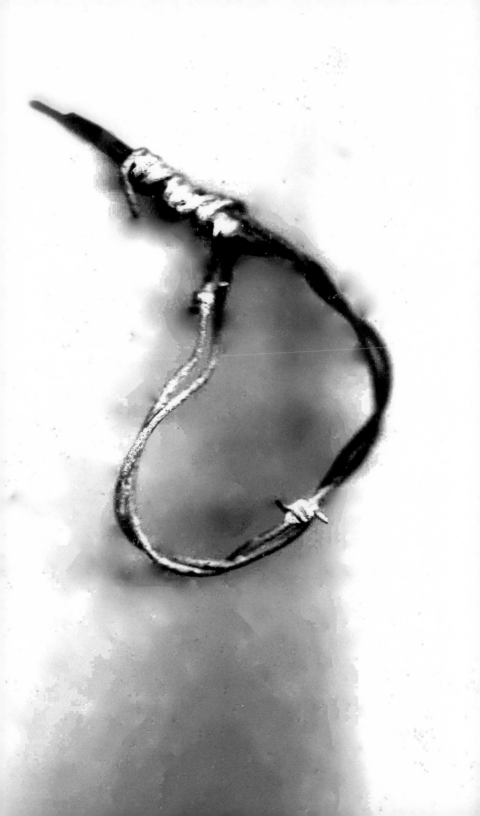

BEAUTIFUL CITY OF TIRZAH

Animals come after my father dies. Dogs. Cats. Ducks. Geese. A goat. A peacock. They wander to our home several years into his absence, appearing on our doorstep, or catching our eye from feedstore cages. Always we take them in. We line our laundry room floor with bath towels, bedsheets, and spare blankets, filling cereal bowls with tap water, and mending cut skin, matted fur, and broken feathers. Then we flick off the light to watch them sleep.

"Strays make the best pets," my mother tells us kids. "They won't leave."

❋

Beggars' Night, 1970. My big brother is late. Again. Our mother said he could play after supper on the ditch bank behind our house, to see if neighbors will give him Halloween candy a day early, but when I peek outside to check on him, the sun has already set, shadows dripping like blue ink from the cottonwoods. But I don't say anything to our mother, who sits in her antique rocker tapping a Russian olive switch on the floor. I scoot on my knees across the hardwood to take my place before living room TV, where my three sisters huddle before the "Movie of the Week," *Dr. No.* It's a school night. We've changed into our flannel pajamas. Our hair is damp from the bath.

"Mom!"

The back door thuds open. My brother clomps through the kitchen breathing hard as if he's been running. Our mother stands, grips the switch, and intercepts him in the dining room. The overhead light flicks on, bright as an interrogation lamp.

"Wait!" my brother pleads. "I found something. Look!"

I scramble to my feet and jockey for position with my sisters. Our brother reaches into his brown corduroy jacket, extracts a small bundle, and opens his hands. A baby bird squints at us.

"An owl," mother says, setting aside her switch. "It's adorable. Where did you find it?"

My brother had been hurrying home along the acequia when he heard a rustling from the bushes. When he slid down the embankment to investigate, he startled a hatchling that skittered through the dirt but couldn't fly. He thought it might have broken its wing, so he scooped it up.

"I looked for the nest but couldn't find it," he says, shifting his weight from one foot to another. "Then I saw its mama by a tree. Someone shot her or something."

Our mother holds the owl to the warmth of her body. It looks up at her, and blinks.

✻

An ornithologist who lives down the street tells my mother we've adopted a screech owl, probably a female, given the description over the phone. Although it's not allowed under city codes, we can probably nurse the chick until she gets stronger. Feed her bits of stew meat, he advises, and later mice. Keep her in a large cage or an enclosed room, and watch out for our cats.

My mother follows every instruction but one: the cage. She wants the owl to fly freely in her home. She retrieves a cardboard box from behind Safeway, lines it with newspapers and old towels, and places a piñon branch inside as a perch. Then she sets the whole thing on the dining room pottery case where our cats can't easily reach.

The owl is the size and shape of an upside-down pear. Her feathers are gray with black-and-white speckles. She has two tufts on her head that look like ears, or horns, and her beak is as sharp and shiny black as her talons. What I like best are her eyes, piercing yellow, the size of dimes. When she looks at me, it's like she's reading my mind, or seeing something I can't. One of my aunts won't meet her gaze. The owl's eyes, she says, are too human.

❋

My mother considers the bird's name carefully. Usually she names the pets after artists she admires, like Toshiro, the Japanese actor, for the silky black-and-white cat. Or sometimes she chooses characters from her favorite films, like Tonya, from *Dr. Zhivago*, for the German shepherd. For the owl, my mother decides on Tirzah.

"Tirzah," she says, savoring the syllables, which break like the morning light through her bedroom window crystals, turquoise and gold. "My little Tirzah."

"What's it mean?" I ask, watching her stroke the bird.

"It's an old name. A religious name. From the Bible."

Later, I look it up in the library: "Tirzah—A city in Palestine, a beautiful place alluded to in the Songs of Solomon ('You are as beautiful, my darling, as Tirzah')."

❋

Each morning, my mother sets the owl's box on the dining room table while she makes breakfast, sketches, or pays bills. Tirzah hops out immediately and waddles over to nibble my mother's pen. If she leaves the room, the owl scurries after her. The only way my mother can finish her chores is to wrap the bird in a washcloth and tuck her in the breast pocket of her denim work shirt. Tirzah remains there for hours, lulled by my mother's heartbeat.

❋

On Sunday evenings, my grandmother, Desolina, stops by our house for pot roast stuffed with garlic. Over supper she grumbles about her childhood in Corrales, growing up among horses, cows, and chickens in a drafty adobe where black widow spiders dropped from the rafters into her tin cup of milk or coffee. She hated every minute of it, she says, chewing with her mouth open, but learned the old ways despite herself. She knows how to bleed a goat, how to age red wine, and how to treat a rattlesnake bite with chewing tobacco. She also knows about spirits.

While my mother collects the supper dishes, I line my toy knights on the kitchen table and listen to the two of them whisper in Spanish about dead relatives. When Desolina catches me eavesdropping— and she always catches me—she laughs under her breath and beckons with an arthritic finger. "Come here, mí hijito," she says, leaning from her chair and clutching a shiny black handbag. Then, in a low raspy voice, she describes the fireballs dancing along the Rio Grande bosque, the footsteps dragging down her hallway at midnight, and the crone who transformed into a banshee to chase her brother home on an acequia near Bernalillo.

"It's true," she says, nodding at my wide eyes, then breaking into a smile of bright red lipstick and crooked teeth. "And did you go to church like I told you?"

When Tirzah flutters by, my grandmother makes the sign of the cross. Owls, she always says, are bad omens, messengers of the night.

"Que fea," she mutters. "Why did you bring that ugly thing in your home?"

My mother shrugs. "I think she's gorgeous."

When Tirzah settles on the back of a kitchen chair across from her, Desolina holds the owl's gaze for a full thirty seconds. Then she slips a glow-in-the-dark rosary from her purse, turns her head, and spits.

❈

Unlike the other kids on the block, I don't go camping. I don't go fishing, boating, or even to Uncle Cliff's Family Land. My mother doesn't like tourists. Doesn't like doing what everyone else does. On the weekends, we go exploring. We pile into her Comet and hit the road. We visit old churches, abandoned graveyards, ghost towns, and adobe ruins, chasing a landscape and culture she says is vanishing before our eyes. She talks to old people, scours the ground for roots and fossils, and collects antique tables and chairs while I run with my siblings through the juniper and ponderosa pine playing *The Last of the Mohicans.*

One Saturday morning washed clean by spring rain, we take my grandfather's pickup north to Truchas, a village so high in the Sangre de Cristos we almost touch the clouds.

In a roadside meadow, my grandfather, Carlos, notices a slice of aspen bark—eight feet long, crescent shaped, with a knothole at one end. My uncle, who's come along for the ride, says it looks like a cobra. I see a dragon. My mother says it has character, so we pitch it in the truck.

Before heading back to Albuquerque, we stop at the tiendita for gas, chile chips, and root beer. The old man behind the counter tells us the bark was cut by lightning a few nights earlier. He saw the flash and heard the boom. This makes my mother smile. Great symbolism, she says.

Back home, she nails the plank across the living room wall. Tirzah notices immediately. She flies from the dining room pottery case and claims the perch as her own, sliding down to the knothole, watching us through the dragon's eye.

✳

My brother finds most of our strays. Or they find him. He'll see a German shepherd digging in the garbage, walk right up, and it'll lick his hand, a friend for life. He has a way with animals, which soothe him in a way no one else can. He was six when our father died. He has the most memories.

We're polar opposites, as our mother likes to say. And she's right. My brother loses his temper like the strike of a match, plays hardball without a glove, and keeps a Mexican switchblade in his drawer. He's always moving, always fidgeting, and always running, as if he's afraid to look over his shoulder. I'm steady, docile, and brooding, like my duck, Hercules, with his blunt beak and orange feet, quite content to never leave his yard.

On weekday afternoons, Tirzah waits by the front window for my brother to return home from school. She hoots when he shuffles through the driveway, flies to his room while he changes from nice clothes into blue jeans, and perches patiently on his shoulder while our mother tethers them together with a strand of yarn—boy's wrist to owl's leg. Task complete, they step outside to straddle his Sting Ray bike. I watch from the front porch as they pull away, Tirzah's eyes swallowing light and motion—the flashing chrome handlebars, the fluttering cottonwood leaf.

"Be careful," our mother shouts, but my brother stands on his pedals anyway, and steers a wide circle under the streetlamp, gathering speed for the lap around the block. Tirzah grips his jacket, and leans into the wind.

❋

The owl isn't my pet, although I'd like her to be. She won't come when I call, perch on my finger, or take meat from my hand, as she does with my mother, uncle, or brother. It's not that I'm afraid of her, exactly. It's more that she's too beautiful to touch. When she does approach me, I get nervous, and she flies away.

One afternoon, though, while I'm doing homework, Tirzah flutters down beside me onto the dining room table.

"Hi, pretty girl," says my mother, who sits beside me sewing a blouse. "Are you thirsty?"

Tirzah waddles up to me, ignoring the water bowl my mother slides forward. I tap the pencil eraser on my teeth.

"Go ahead," my mother says. "Pet her. She won't bite."

"I know, but she doesn't like me."

"That's not true. Just scratch her head. She loves that. Rub in little circles."

I extend the pencil. Tirzah flinches, eyes wide, preparing to fly.

"See?" I say, withdrawing my hand. "She hates me."

"Wait," my mother whispers. "Try again. Slower."

I inch the eraser forward until it touches the owl's head. Tirzah squints but stays put.

"Use your finger," my mother says. "Good. Just like that. See how funny it feels? Like a Ping-Pong ball?"

Tirzah closes her eyes and leans into the pressure. The more she relaxes, the more I relax. After a few minutes, the owl curls her toes and rolls onto her side, asleep.

❈

My grandfather Carlos visits us on his the way home from the highway crew. At sixty-five, after raising nine children and working all his life in construction, he insists on holding a job. He nods hello to us, settles into a corner rocker, and hangs his gray fedora on his bony knee while my mother fetches him a cold Coors longneck.

Carlos doesn't talk much. He prefers to watch, listen, and absorb the warmth of a family life he never had as a boy. His father died when he was eight. When his mother remarried, her husband refused to raise another man's son, so she sent him to a boarding school in Santa Fe. He ran away with a friend soon afterward, walking a hundred miles through the Rio Puerco badlands to the mining village of Marquez, where he worked odd jobs. Carlos slept in arroyos, caves, and abandoned barns during that trek through the chamisal and cholla. On those lonely nights, owls watched him from the junipers, bathed in silver moonlight.

One night, Tirzah glides down to his armrest from her aspen perch. When Carlos extends his gnarled finger, she hops on. He raises her to his nose, and smiles.

❈

Each winter, our house fills with the sweet scent of piñon. We have no fireplace or wood-burning stove, so my mother sprinkles trading-post incense over the steel grate of our living room floor furnace. It reminds her of childhood on the rancho, she says, crumbling sawdust between her fingers, sparks swirling before her eyes. As a girl, she stoked the potbelly stove in her grandmother's kitchen. Piñon smoke reminds her of black coffee in tin cups, cotton quilts, and crackling orno flames. Piñon smoke takes her back, she says. All the way back.

When my mother leaves to prepare supper, I take her place on the furnace vent, standing in the hot current until my blue jeans burn my legs. As Tirzah glides by, white smoke curling from her wings, I imagine I'm soaring through the clouds beside her, drifting like an apparition above the antique tables, brass lamps, Navajo rugs, and broken clay pots, haunting this room forever.

❋

On nights before art show openings, I sleep to the hiss of my uncle's propane torch and the click of his sculptor's tools. He's the baby in my mother's family, fourteen years her junior. He moved in with us four years after my father died because my mother didn't feel safe alone with five children on the rural edge of northwest Albuquerque. She also wanted a male role model for my brother and me, although my uncle was barely out of his teens. He listens to The Doors, Jimi Hendrix, and Country Joe & the Fish, wears a wizard beard and shoulder-length hair, and walks barefoot everywhere, even in the mountains. I think he looks like George Harrison stepping onto the crosswalk of my mother's favorite album, *Abbey Road*, but my grandmother thinks he looks like Jesus. Desolina wants him to be a priest, to help atone for family sins, but instead he becomes an artist. With needle-nose pliers and rods of Pyrex glass, he creates intricate figurines of Hopi eagle dancers, Mexican vaqueros, and Navajo shepherds, then mounts them on driftwood and volcanic rock. I watch him from my pillow with his Einstein hair and welder's glasses, crafting icy figures from fire. Tirzah perches above his worktable, drawn, as I am, to his clear blue flame.

❋

My mother wants to bless our pets. Although she left the Catholic Church a few years after my father died, she wants protection for our strays. So, on a warm Sunday in February, we load the ducks, geese, peacock, goat, and owl into our Comet and attend the outdoor ceremony.

We stand in line behind a dozen puppies, kitties, gerbils, and bunnies. The priest chuckles from a white gazebo as he sprinkles holy water. When our turn arrives, he stops mid-motion and appraises us behind silver-rimmed eyeglasses. My brother slouches before the dais, arms folded, Tirzah on his shoulder. I kneel beside the black Nubian goat, which suckles from its baby bottle. My oldest sister cradles the peacock, while the other two hold ducks and geese. Our mother lingers on the steps, eyes hidden behind Jackie O sunglasses. We're long-haired, tie-dyed, and proud of it, in full bloom eight years after my father's funeral, surrounded by the animals that brought new life into our home. Parishioners scowl. A poodle yaps. A news photographer snaps our portrait. After a pause, the priest mumbles a prayer. The next day, we make the front page.

❈

Tirzah surprises us. When one of the dogs slinks through the house, she contracts her feathers, squints, and becomes as thin as a dry juniper branch, invisible against the gray aspen plank. She changes direction in mid-flight, as well, hovering in place like a helicopter, swiveling her head, and returning silently the way she came. She's also a stone-cold hunter. When we place a chunk of stew meat on her perch, she puffs to twice her normal size, dilates her pupils, and pounces. She thumps the meat several times, then flings it to the floor. Yellow eyes blazing, talons scratching hardwood, she stalks her meal like a panther. Finding it, she opens her beak and swallows it whole.

❈

During the day the sun is too bright for the owl's sensitive eyes, so she seeks dark corners to sleep in. One morning, when the temperature hits eighty-nine, my middle sister reaches into the hall closet to flick on the swamp cooler, but leaves the door ajar. The chain for the overhead bulb is broken, so the closet is always pitch black.

Tirzah, gazing toward the opening from her perch, flutters atop the closet door. I hold my breath. My sister calls our mother. Normally, the closet is off limits to us kids. We try to shoo Tirzah away, but she won't budge. She just stares into the cool abyss. After a moment, she lowers her head and hops inside. From then on, the hall closet becomes her sanctuary. To fetch her, I must reach into the darkness, brushing my father's things.

✻

My brother finds another stray, a baby meadowlark that had fallen from a cottonwood into an alfalfa field near his school. He can't find the nest, so he once again tucks the orphan under his arm and carries it home. Our mother swaddles the chick in a washcloth, fetches some old newspapers, and phones the ornithologist. I watch her fill an eyedropper with water and hold it to the bird's beak while cradling the receiver in the crook of her neck.

She adores meadowlarks, she says after hanging up. As a girl in Corrales she often woke to the song of meadowlarks in the apple orchards across the road.

"It was so beautiful," she tells me, puckering her lips to whistle. "But sad, too."

She retrieves an extra birdcage from the back porch, places the chick inside, and covers the wire dome with a sheet, as the ornithologist instructed. Standing on her toes, she sets the bundle on the pottery case again, away from the cats. Tirzah watches from the living room perch.

The next morning, I hear my mother gasp. In the dining room I find her holding the cage. In the center of the shredded paper lies the meadowlark, wet with blood.

"Poor little thing," she cries, swatting a tabby off the table. "See what you did!"

My uncle joins us, examines the bird, and concludes that its skull has been crushed. He checks the birdcage for damage. Finding none, he snatches up the cat and holds its paw to the wire bars, but its arm is too thick to fit through. Stumped, he searches the house for clues. On the aspen perch, he discovers a few flecks of wet gray fuzz.

After retrieving Tirzah from the hall closet, he holds her tight with one hand and uses the other to extend one of her long bony legs, which slips neatly into the cage, within easy reach of where the meadowlark had slept.

"You dirty rat!" my uncle says, holding the owl to his face. "Did you kill that poor little bird?"

Tirzah bites his thumb, wriggles away, and flutters back to her living room roost, where she scowls at us the rest of the day. She won't even come to my mother.

❄

I have no bed or room of my own. For more than a year I sleep on an aluminum cot beside the antique church pew in the living room. My mother buys me Snoopy sheets to make me feel better, but I hate that cot, sliding it down the hall each night. The foam mattress smells like dirty socks. The joints pinch my skin. Be patient, my mother says. When I'm ten, she'll restore one of the iron frames on the porch. Soon I'll join my uncle and brother in the boys' room.

When she switches off the floor lamp and the ten o'clock news, I'm alone. I lie back under the silver glow of the curbside streetlamp with the clicks from the vintage clock and the creaks of old walls settling in. From the haze of half sleep, I sense Tirzah awaken. I hear scratching. Feel the weight of eyes. Catch a whiff of closet mothballs. But when I snap awake and sit up, there's only a whisper, an echo, a slight disturbance of air.

❄

The longer she stays with us, the more stir-crazy Tirzah seems to become. Every few weeks, she flies into the broad living room window, unable to see the glass, confused when she can't pass through. My mother draws the curtains and replaces the drapes with bamboo shades, but whenever a sparrow darts by outside, Tirzah pursues it, straight into the glass. My uncle, fearing the owl will crack her skull or break the window, nails a row of Russian olive branches along the outside frame. Tirzah settles before the window on a chair back, gazing through the bars.

One afternoon, the owl goes missing. She's not on her perch, in the hall closet, or in the back rooms. I search under the beds, behind the bookshelves, inside cabinets. I search with my siblings for an hour, but we can't find her. My mother sits stiffly in her rocker, jaw muscle flexing.

"She's gone," she mutters. "I know she is. One of you brats must have left the front door open again. How many times have I told you to close that door?"

My uncle thumps across the floor rechecking the tables and shelves. When one of the dogs slinks by, he kicks it.

"Where's the flashlight? Who took my flashlight?"

I stand with my sisters in the dining room trying to make myself small. I didn't leave the door open. Didn't do anything. But I feel like I did, like I always do when one of our pets is missing or injured, like something that happened a long time ago is about to happen again.

"Don't stand there," my mother says. "Look again."

My little sister begins to cry.

Above the scrape and knock of searching, we hear it: "Hoo."

"Hush!" my mother says, head cocked. "Listen."

"Hoo."

We turn to the pottery case, to a Pueblo water bowl on a back shelf. In it, glaring over the rim, is Tirzah, who settled inside to nap, but woke during our commotion.

My mother rushes forward. "Tirzah!"

My sisters giggle. My uncle snaps a photo.

I hesitate before joining them. I don't like what I see in the owl's eyes. She appears wary, worried, as if seeing my family for the first time.

✻

We're late returning home from a day in the Jemez Mountains. The sky burns orange and red. We race the shadows home, but arrive in darkness. My uncle flicks on the house lights while my mother sparks the floor furnace.

Tirzah, who hasn't eaten since morning, hoots from her aspen perch. My mother opens the refrigerator, scans the shelves, but finds no stew meat, only breakfast steak. She checks the clock. Safeway has just closed. The breakfast steak is fresh, so she chops it up for the owl.

The next day, Tirzah won't eat or drink. She barely flies. The ornithologist asks my mother to read the steak label to him over the phone. She does, in a whisper.

It's just what he feared, the ornithologist tells her. The breakfast steak has a chemical protein that stew meat doesn't. Tirzah was poisoned.

My mother paces the living room. My sisters and I pray to St. Francis of Assisi.

The following morning, I find my mother sobbing at the dining room table. She'd woken up early to check on Tirzah, and found the bird motionless in the water bowl. The thirsty owl had leaned over the rim and fallen inside. Too weak to climb out, Tirzah drowned.

※

My uncle digs deep in the backyard cactus garden, grunting white puffs of steam. My mother stands beside him holding a shoebox. In it lies the owl, wrapped in a washcloth. The air is still, the sky pink and yellow.

Wordless, my uncle tosses the shovel clanging to the hard ground. He and my mother shuffle away, heads down, seeking driftwood or river rocks to mark the grave. I stare into the hole, another absence I will never fill.

After a minute my uncle returns with a piñon branch. My mother lowers the shoebox into the red sand. We bury Tirzah among the prickly pear, yucca and, chamisal, beside the goat, the peacock, and the mallard named Hercules.

WHITE

CREAM

With a cup of strong coffee and five packets of creamer, I can approximate the skin tone of the nine members of my mother's family.

MILK

I never see the shadow or the red carton flash, and even when the pint of milk explodes against the head of my wheat-haired friend I'm late to understand what the Chicano boy means when he curses from the sidewalk of my junior high cafeteria, "Shit. Missed that honky."

DOUGH

I watch my mother in the kitchen table glow of our Albuquerque home, rolling pin thumping, windows steamed, kneading flour, soda, and salt as effortlessly as the Spanish and English blend on her tongue.

"¿De veras?" my grandmother asks.

"Oh, sí," my mother replies. "Every word."

I eat my tortillas hot and whole and plain, nourishing myself on the ingredients as if they really were my bread.

LARD

My mother has her own philosophy about beans. Instead of spooning in the traditional curl of Snowcap pig's fat, she adds bay leaves, olive oil, sea salt, and garlic. She cooks her pintos all day over a low gas flame, in a Pyrex pot, until the broth bubbles a rich murky brown. When an aunt, cousin, or neighbor visits for supper, they

always frown from their first sip. "Good," they say. "But different."
To which my mother replies, "Exactly."

PEARL

During World War II, around the time of the Zoot Suit Riots, my mother lived in Los Angeles. From her apartment window she watched pachucos strut along the boulevard in their shoulder-padded jackets, pleated trousers, and wide-brim hats of red, green, blue, and yellow, as proud as tropical birds.

One summer her uncle Gilo visited from her grandparents' rancho in Corrales. He was the baby in her mother's family, spoiled rotten because of his fair skin, blond hair, and sage green eyes, the image of his father, who cherished his Spanish blood. Gilo had never been to the big city, so my mother took him out for ice cream. They strolled hand in hand along the sidewalk, turning heads as they went, she in her schoolgirl plaids and he in his Western shirt, Dorothy and the Scarecrow in the Land of Oz. Several pachucos blocked their path.

"Where are you going, gringo?" the biggest one asked.

The pachucos circled them.

"Who do you think you are? The Lone Ranger?"

The big one flicked off Gilo's cowboy hat.

"Hi ho, Silver!"

My mother turned to run. Gilo stammered, "My name's Perea." In Spanish, he explained he was visiting from New Mexico. If they didn't believe him, he'd fetch his uncle.

The pachucos fell over themselves laughing. They punched Gilo's arm, pinched his cheek, and escorted him to the ice cream shop. For the rest of his visit, they treated Gilo like royalty, like a movie star, like a jewel.

EGGSHELL

Ricky Sandoval pins me by the throat against a C-Building locker, the combination lock spinning beside my head, and slaps me on one cheek, then the other, until my composure cracks, my eyes water, and my face burns red.

"See?" he says. "That's all you need. A little color."

SCAR

The razor is too dull to cut, so I scratch a fingernail on the back of my left hand hoping my big brother will see. He yanks me off the front porch anyway and into the kitchen where he and his fatherless friends have found a better way to scar—a curtain pin heated orange on the gas range and pressed to the tender fold between thumb and forefinger, into the shape of a cross, into the symbol of belonging he's seen on brown Chicano fists. He holds my arm tight against the Formica counter while I close my eyes and still see the blue flame. A vodka shot. A cold water blast. I stand beside him as our matching crucifixes swell with blood. Afterward, we raid vegetable gardens, set pampas plumes alight, and bust phonebooths until glass drips from our denim jackets like rain. I pick the scab to keep the scar alive, but my cross fades first, swallowed by pale skin.

LIQUID PAPER

"No. We are in *not* Mexican," my mother says.

"Chicano?" I ask.

"No," she says, snickering.

"Spanish?"

"No."

"Then what do I say on my report?"

"Don't say anything."

"How about Irish? Like Dad."

"He wasn't Irish. He was Scottish-French."

"Wasn't your grandmother Italian? I thought that's where I got my red hair."

"Your hair isn't red. It's auburn. And if you want to know the truth, my family's Basque."

"How do you spell it?"

ASPIRIN

Fourteen in the backyard weeds among the horseflies and cicadas with my bath towel and baby oil, shirtless under the hundred-degree sun. It's late August, two weeks to remake myself for my sophomore year at Valley High. My head pounds. My ears buzz. My navel pools with sweat.

An hour later, a rash breaks across my torso. Second-degree burns, the doctor tells my mother on the phone. An allergic reaction to the sun. His prescription: ice cubes, a cold compress, Noxzema, and Bayer tablets for the pain.

I spend two days in bed raking my fingernails over itchy lubricated skin. It's okay, I tell my mother and snickering sisters. When the swelling stops, maybe I'll tan.

FLUORESCENT

Brendon Jefferson is the only black kid in tenth grade PE. He dribbles two basketballs simultaneously, leaps above the rim, dunks them both. I watch from the sidelines, envious.

One morning during wrestling, we sit side by side on the mat with the soccer captain and the driver of a low-slung Monte Carlo, hugging our knees while the coach pairs us into matches. Brendon looks at each of us, then pokes his thigh, the soccer player's thigh, and the low-rider's thigh.

"Check this out," he says. "I'm black. He's yellow. He's brown. And you . . ."

He jabs my skin, bloodless under fluorescent lights.

"You're just white!"

He rolls onto his back, laughing.

We wrestle to a draw.

LOTION

"Shake well before using. Blend evenly over freshly cleansed skin. Apply sparingly around elbows, knees and ankles. Wash hands with soap immediately after use. Avoid contact with clothing until dry. The Sheer Bronzer is a temporary color. It should not stain clothing and should wash off in water. Therefore, you should wait to go swimming until after you have showered. Your sunless tan will develop in two to four hours and will last for days. Reapply as needed to maintain or deepen color."

GHOST

After college I attend a National Association of Hispanic Journalists convention in Dallas. I linger among the beige cubicles while other reporters and editors brush past me with résumés and business cards. When I approach, they study my face, squint at my nametag, and turn away. Several hours into the job fair, with few interviews and even fewer prospects, I duck into a men's room, flip over my badge, and scribble in my mother's maiden name, Candelaria. Back in the main arena, recruiters smile, hands extend, appointments open.

I walk through walls.

BONE

So what do I need to know, asks the man in camouflage fatigues, the man with the Emiliano Zapata mustache, who has dug his friend into a black soil bunker in Tierra Amarilla. What do I need to know about a sixty-one-year-old farmer who refuses to leave his pasture because development lawyers have swindled away his land grant? What do I need to know that the automatic rifle in the grip of the farmer's fifteen-year-old son can't tell me? What do I need to know that will help an Anglo reporter like me understand?

"But, I'm not an Anglo," I say.

"Oh, no?" he asks, teeth flashing. "What are you then?"

I start to tell him, but the words stick in my throat.

LIGHTBULB

"A Chicano," explains the sculptor, the activist, the co-founder of the Denver multicultural arts council, "is someone who is born in the United States but has a blood mixture of Aztec and Spanish. A Chicano is a person with one foot in one culture and one foot in another culture who resists being forced to choose. A Chicano is a person trying to define themselves for themselves. A Chicano is a person seeking their true identity."

"I guess that makes me a Chicano," I say, touching my pale cheek.

"Me, too," she says laughing. "And I was born in Mexico."

LILY

My wife's youngest sister is the darkest among her four siblings, with a skin tone of a coconut. She lives in a suburban home decorated with artificial plants, Ethan Allen furniture, and still-life prints. She cooks green chile enchiladas with Campbell's cream-of-mushroom soup and drives her kids to soccer camp in an American-made SUV. My wife and I choose a bungalow in the Hispanic part of Denver, clutter our walls with New Mexican folk art, prefer our green chile straight, and encourage our son and daughter to learn Spanish.

During a visit to Albuquerque, I sit with my sister-in-law under a poolside umbrella, watching our kids splash and sparkle. Her son and daughter glow bronze under the August sun. My daughter burns pink.

"I can't get over it," my sister-in-law says. "Your daughter is so . . . white."

COTTON

I dry off my five-year-old daughter after swim lessons. Goosebumps break across her thighs. At the edge of her one-piece, I notice a darkening of skin tone.

"Look, honey. You're getting some color."

"No, Dad," she says, hiding her leg behind the cotton towel. "I don't want a tan."

BLANK

NOTE: Please Answer BOTH questions, numbers 7 *and* 8.

7) Are you Spanish/Hispanic/Latino? (Mark the "no" box
   if not Spanish/Hispanic/Latino)
   ☐ No, not Spanish/Hispanic/Latino
   ☐ Yes, Puerto Rican
   ☐ Yes, Cuban
   ☐ Yes, Mexican, Mexican-American, Chicano
   ☐ Yes, other Spanish/Hispanic/Latino—Print
      here:_____

8) What is your race? Mark one
   - ☐ Black, African-American, Negro
   - ☐ American Indian, Alaskan Native
   - ☐ Pacific Islander, Asian
   - ☐ White
   - ☐ Some other race. Print here:_____

AMONG THE BROKEN ANGELS

She draws me in with her voice, her story voice, breath-less, distant, elusive as smoke.

"Death has a face," my mother says. "Did you know that?"

I sit on my front porch steps in Denver sketching a shrine for Dia de los Muertos, for my father, and she switches the conversation from folk art to her childhood, pulling me through the phone line into her world of se-crets.

"The body stiffens, the back arches, the toes point, and the face makes all these expressions. Then the mouth opens wide and the eyes open wide, and all of a sudden, the body lets loose and relaxes. Something just . . . gives."

Then she stops, as she always does, mistaking my si-lence for disbelief, and I slide into the space between what she says and what I see.

❈

We drive, my mother and I, into the Rio Puerco bad-lands, a sun-baked table of cactus and volcanic rock six-ty miles northwest of Albuquerque. We seek the roots of her stories, the villages of her youth, Corrales, San Luis, Guadalupe, lands that haunt her, that haunt me. We watch the sand change from cinnamon to chocolate to raspberry to bone. Pass cliffs as sharp as dinosaur spines. Read symbols and metaphors, the cholla twisted into a crucifix, the cry of a raven or a baby. Tires crunch, stones bounce, dust swirls around us like ghosts. All morning, into the afternoon, wasp on the dashboard, driftwood in the trunk, my mother and I go back.

※

Wind blew from the north, lashing the gnarled gray branches of the cottonwoods until they twisted and writhed like witches. Above White Mesa, thunderheads bruised the sky.

Juan Mora stomped on the accelerator, and his flatbed tore along the wagon trail leading east from his Rio Puerco village. He was running out of time. And he knew it. He'd left the headgate open again, and if he didn't get to his fields soon, his meager crop of pinto beans would drown in the torrent of rainwater set to roar through the acequias like a stampede. He'd had a string of bad harvests lately, and with the hot breath of the Dust Bowl bearing down from Oklahoma and Texas, he couldn't survive another. Shovels clattered in the truck bed. His oldest son, Vidal, bounced on the seat beside him, slamming his head on the roof. Juan didn't notice. His eyes were fixed on the anvil cloud sliding in from Jemez Pueblo. In ten minutes, maybe fifteen, he'd lose it all.

Juan braked at the edge of his shallow furrows, gravel spraying from his truck tires like a shotgun blast. He hopped out, grabbed a shovel, and thrust it at Vidal.

"Fix that break. At the north end. Hurry!"

Vidal sprinted away while Juan made for the headgate at the south, his lanky frame loping along the banks of a canal he'd dug only four years earlier, when he gazed into the buckskin folds of the valley and saw a shimmer he mistook for a promise. His boots fell heavily on the thick sand, and for a moment he was dreaming, running in place, arms pumping, sinking deeper into a land that would not be nourished with anything less than blood. At last he reached the large iron wheel regulating the flow of irrigation water. He gritted his teeth and turned, with all his strength he turned, rotation after screeching rotation, until his chest heaved, his arms burned, and the heavy plate sank into the mud. He'd made it, he told himself. For once in his life, he'd made it.

Juan wiped his forehead with his shirtsleeve, rested the shovel on his shoulder, and glanced back at Vidal. As he opened his mouth to call his son, the wind gusted, sending his straw cowboy hat zigzagging over the fields.

"Shoot," he grumbled, and started after it.

Fifty yards away, Vidal bent over a breech, scooping silt with his hands, cold, tired, cursing under his breath. Everyone knew the storm was coming, he thought. Why did his father have to soak his fields so long? Why did he always wait until the last minute? Couldn't he do anything right?

Then a flash—and a BOOM!

Vidal tumbled onto his side, ears ringing, enveloped by the odor of burned hair.

"Papá?"

He pushed himself up and scanned the fields, but he couldn't see his father.

"Papá!"

He scrambled toward the headgate but slipped and fell, his mouth filling with the coppery taste of blood. Sloshing ahead on all fours, he saw a yellow curl hidden among the squat green leaves: his father's hat. As Vidal reached for it, other shapes took form—a denim sleeve, an arm, a pair of overalls, a man on his back.

"Papá!"

It began to rain.

❋

Sixty miles southeast, in the village of Corrales, Abenicio Perea, my great-grandfather, dozed off in his broad iron bed when a voice whirled into his room.

"Estoy muerto!"

Abenicio reached over to shake his wife.

"It's Juan," he whispered. "Juan Mora."

"I hear it," Adelaida said. "Be quiet!"

The voice whipped around them, once, twice, then tore down the road to the adobe home of Carlos Candelaria, my grandfather, Juan's brother-in-law and best friend.

"Estoy muerto!"

Carlos covered his head with a bedsheet while his wife, Desolina, used a pillow to shield their infant daughter, my mother, who slept between them.

"Estoy muerto! I'm dead!"

The foot of the bed rose ten inches off the floorboards before slamming down hard. Desolina closed her eyes, sat up straight, and made the sign of the cross.

"May God forgive your sins!" she shouted. "Rest in peace! Leave us alone!"

Then nothing. The patter of rain on the sunflowers beneath the window.

Carlos listened a good three minutes before slipping on his boots and rushing outside to investigate. Desolina called after him, checked the baby, and followed.

My mother remained in bed asleep.

A spirit had come to them, an angry, anguished spirit, and yet she remained calm, content, dreaming.

✳

My car rolls toward the stone archway of the Corrales cemetery, gravel popping beneath the tires. Before we enter, my mother reaches over and places her hand on mine.

"Wait," she says, slipping a crystal rosary from her purse. "We have to pray."

"Pray?"

"So a spirit won't attach to us. A malevolent spirit."

She lowers her head, but pauses, waiting for me to join her, then proceeding slowly when I don't. "Holy Michael the Archangel, defend us in battle. Be our protection against the devil. May God rebuke him. We humbly pray."

I listen closely, respectfully, but I don't know the prayer, or many others. I don't tell her what I'm thinking, either, that part of me wants a spirit to come, not a malevolent spirit, but a gentle guide, like my father, who will speak to me as he speaks to her, in dreams.

"Amen." My mother smiles thinly, makes the sign of the cross, smooths her auburn hair, and slips outside.

Watching her enter the camposanto, I wonder again what she knows, what she sees, and how she has learned to brush aside the veil of death. I cut the engine and follow.

The October sun warms my face. The breeze carries the smell of dust and weeds. Dogs bark. Sparrows twitter. A hawk slices through the turquoise sky. Careful not to wake the dead, I tread lightly among the uneven rows of simple earthen graves, some tended, others not, past hand-hewn crosses of splintered wood and saints of crumbling concrete. The sand sparkles with the remnants of votive candles, shards of orange, violet, green, and pink, sprinkled like lost jewels among the prickly pear and black widow spiders. Roses, carnations, tulips, and daisies, plastic and living, color the headstones with bursts of red, yellow, blue, and gold.

This ground is beautiful to me, so different from the urban cemeteries with their hissing sprinklers and carpeted lawns, so different from the military grounds in Santa Fe, where my father is buried. When I stand among those identical white markers laid as tight as false teeth, I'm numb to my emotions. But here, among the broken angels, I feel all the sorrow and love I've tried so hard to summon for him.

"It's so powerful," I say, joining my mother at a cement slab adorned with red tulips. "So much . . . passion."

"Yes," she says, kneeling before the square marble headstone. "The people here are very devoted."

Leaning forward, I read the chiseled inscription: "Juan Mora. Born 25 Dec. 1904. Died 10 Jun 1936."

Juan Mora. Instantly, I'm transported back into my mother's story, into my vision of it, into the adobe room where she slept between her parents as the spirit raged.

"So, Grandma and Granddad both heard this voice?" I ask, returning to our earlier conversation, pulling her with me through time. "This . . . ghost?"

"Oh, yes," my mother says, straightening a crooked flower. "They all told the same story. And they all said I slept through the whole thing."

"Were you ever afraid? Growing up like that?"

She laughs. Shakes her head.

"Oh, no. People were religious back then. Not like they are today. They understood that spirits are all around us. When I was a girl there weren't many phones in the country. When someone died, they told you in other ways. A chair moved, or a picture fell. Once, when I was staying with my grandmother, she came into the kitchen one morning and said, 'I dreamt of my best friend last night. I saw her in a coffin. Get your things. We're going to Villa Nueva.' And sure enough, when we got there, her friend had died. That kind of thing happened all the time. It's called a presentimiento. A premonition. Something you feel in your heart."

❋

My mother was five. She stood in the darkened hallway of an uncle's adobe in La Ventana, peering through a half-closed door. Kerosene lamps flickered inside the bedroom, painting the walls with amber light. Through the opening, she watched her grandmother and two midwives attending a pregnant cousin.

Something was wrong. My mother knew it. She'd heard it in her uncle's voice as he mumbled from the porch step of her grandparents' Corrales rancho an hour earlier. She'd seen it her grandmother's frown as the old woman packed a satchel with curandera's herbs, bandages, holy water, and jars of salve. She'd sensed it in the autumn air as soon as she'd set foot in the drafty corridor. Something was wrong. And she was afraid.

Many times she'd accompanied her grandmother to pray at the bedsides of the sick and dying, to offer the potent blessings of an innocent, but she'd never been asked to remain outside a room for so long, and never alone.

She placed her fingertips on the door and pushed.

Her cousin screamed—a high-pitched wail from deep inside her belly, fire and wind, anger and anguish.

My mother jumped back, stumbled.

Her cousin screamed again, then again, louder and louder until her cries filled the shadowy hall.

My mother covered her ears. Slid down the wall.

Then it stopped.

Silence settled around her, heavy as a cloak.

The door creaked open with a shaft of smoke and light.

The old women filed out one by one, faces as hard as walnuts, slick with sweat and tears.

My mother reached out, but her grandmother waved her off, "Wait here," then disappeared down the corridor.

Twisting the hem of her dress, my mother turned toward the muffled voices from the kitchen-her grandmother, the midwives, her uncle. A bottle clinked. A chair skidded across the floor. Her uncle growled, sobbed.

Unable to wait any longer, my mother stepped forward to join them, but paused before the bedroom door.

Her cousin lay back, unmoving, face white as the moon.

My mother tiptoed inside.

The young woman gazed silently upward, eyes wide with surprise, at a circle of lamp light on the ceiling.

"Are you okay?"

Approaching the bed, my mother noticed the slick red linen and the wadded towels between her cousin's legs. Then she saw it, wrapped in blankets at her cousin's side, a newborn, perfect as a doll, skin as ruddy as a plum.

"What are you doing?" Adelaida appeared just then in the doorway, holding fresh linen and a basin bowl of water.

My mother wheeled around. "Can I hold him?"

"What?" Her grandmother scowled. "Who?"

"The baby. Can I hold the baby?"

Adelaida glanced at the stillborn, her face softening with a sigh. "No, mija. He's gone, pobrecito. Your cousin, too. Now go wait outside. I won't be long. Promise."

The midwives slipped into the room, ignoring my mother. One

peeled away the bloody bedsheets while the other placed a brass crucifix on the dead woman's pillow. Adelaida set the bowl on the nightstand and began to bathe the body.

My mother turned to leave, but hesitated, and reached toward the baby. He was cold, so cold, so she bundled his feet, pulled the blankets to his chin, and kissed his cheek.

❋

An hour into our drive, my mother and I stand at the edge of the Rio Puerco, a meandering trickle of brown water its Spanish name, dirty river. It's almost dry now, but over time it has cut a ragged gouge thirty feet into the sand and sediment, cracking away from us as if the earth has split at our feet. On the plains beyond, plumes of chamisal and buffalo grass ripple in the wind like jackrabbit fur. Miles farther in the distance, the blue volcanic hump of El Cabezon, the hat, and the squat adobe homes, trailers, and white propane tanks of Lucero, San Luis, and Guadalupe. My mother kneels to gather a handful of stones for her collection. I do the same.

She traveled here often as a girl with her father and grandfather, she says, delivering apples, squash, green chile, and sweet corn from Corrales to the badlands. She'd hug the produce barrels in the buckboard wagon and later the flatbed Ford, watching the spoked wheels turn.

"It's so peaceful here," she says, breathing in the smell of hot dust and dry grass. "Healing."

I feel it too, the solitude, the serenity, and yet, I can still hear the echoes of her stories, stories I inhabit without meaning to. I can still hear her cousin's scream. Still see my mother with the dead baby. I want to reach back decades and pull her from that hallway, hold her, comfort her, apologize for what she was made to see.

"How horrible," I say, breaking the silence, calling her back to the bedroom in La Ventana, the Spanish word for window. "What was your grandmother thinking showing you that?"

"Horrible?" She frowns. "Oh, no. You've got it all wrong. In those days, people were very spiritual. Very religious. They didn't get angry or blame God whenever someone died. They accepted it as part of life. That's just the way it was back then. Every family lost someone."

✱

They were three years apart, my mother and her younger sister Ernestina. They wore the same hand-sewn dresses, played with the same rag dolls, slept in the same iron bed. When Ernestina's lips turned purple after a game of chase, my mother sat beside her until breath returned. When Ernestina snapped awake after a nightmare, my mother held her hand.

In July 1944 my mother's family returned to Albuquerque after several years in Los Angeles, where her father had found work in the wartime shipyards. Doctors advised against the move home, fearing that the thin desert air would strain Ernestina's heart, which had been scarred in infancy by rheumatic fever. The family returned anyway because Ernestina's health worsened with the pollen and smog of California. In New Mexico, her parents hoped, with farm-fresh vegetables and dry heat, she might improve. But after two weeks, Ernestina couldn't cross a room without collapsing.

One muggy morning while staying with their aunt Molly, Ernestina sat in a guest-room rocker, limp as the Raggedy Ann in her lap, watching my mother and their older sister change the bedding, which unfurled like wings in the bright sunlight.

"Look," Ernestina said eyes wide, pointing to the bedside. "A woman."

"Where?" My mother followed her line of sight.

"There. A beautiful woman."

Their older sister scowled. "Stop pretending."

"I'm not," Ernestina cried. "There *is* a woman!"

Their mother poked her head into the room. "Hush. Stop fighting. Why aren't you done yet?"

When Ernestina explained, the blood drained from Desolina's face. "Don't say that," she said, fearing her daughter had seen an angel sent to usher her through an impending death. "Don't ever say that. Now get back to work."

The girls finished in silence.

A few nights later, thunderheads burst over the Sandia Mountains. Mist hung like smoke. Ernestina fought for every breath. My mother, unable to comfort her, called out for their father, Carlos, who cradled his frail daughter on the bedside.

Carlos loved all his children, but Ernestina was his favorite. They shared the same dark eyes, thin smile, and melancholy laugh. Each day after work he brought her a treat of some kind, a stick of gum, an apple, a new penny.

All night the rain pounded. Carlos held his daughter, whispering into her hair. While her fever spiked, her skin paled, and her heart finally stopped, he held her as tight as a fist. My mother sat beside them, weeping like the sky.

At dawn, my mother helped her grandmother prepare the body. She dipped a cotton cloth into a porcelain bowl, then washed Ernestina's eyelids, chin, nose, fingers, toes. She whispered prayers. Lit votive candles. Dressed Ernestina in a creamy satin Communion gown. And when the family gathered around the iron bed for the velorio, my mother carried the basin bowl into the bathroom, held the lip to the sink, and poured the water through her fingers.

❋

The wind is constant in San Luis, a low moan through barbed-wire fences stitching the valley together like seems on a gunnysack. My mother and I pass abandoned shacks, dilapidated corrals, crumbling stone walls, sagging outhouses, empty doorways, remnants of hard lives worn away.

Before leaving, I park at the village church, a whitewashed adobe box standing sentry on the edge of the plains. I peek in the windows, but it's too dark to see inside. I rattle the door, but it's locked. Frowning, my mother leads me to the camposanto a dozen yards away, pausing at the iron gate to examine a wooden cross slipped into the cross-hatched wire. A single grave remains visible—a pile of stones and a cluster of sun-bleached plastic carnations. No headstone. No crucifix. Just a dented bucket for a marker.

Head low, my mother kneels to touch a lavender aster poking up through the hard-packed sand.

"It is so desolate here," she whispers. "So unforgiving. But they carved a life. They endured. They had rules and they stuck to them. If you stole or drank you were cast out, ostracized. And they had faith, too. It wasn't unusual in those days to see a big strong man like my grandfather drop to his knees and pray. To survive, they needed to believe."

I gaze out across the cemetery grounds. A crow glides above the tufts of chamisal, struggling against the wind.

"Some people can't handle the isolation," she says standing, shoulders square. "But I'd live here if I could."

Watching her against the backdrop of sandstone and scrub brush, her skin as weathered as adobe bricks, her hair as dry as buffalo grass, I believe she would.

She grins at me, nods, and pockets a fossilized stone.

"I didn't know you watched your sister die," I say, probing again. "That must have been hard on you."

"Yes," she says softly. "We were very close. But your granddad took it the worst. He made the headstone himself. Out of concrete. Before he died, he made me promise to tend her grave. And I do. Every year I visit Corrales to pull weeds and water the flowers. He wanted me to plant purple irises, his favorite, but they couldn't take the direct sun, so I planted a prickly pear instead. Each spring it's loaded with big, beautiful blossoms. Bright fuchsia."

"Do you still think about her? Dream about her?"

"Sometimes. But listen. You're supposed to pray for them. If a spirit comes, you forgive them of their sins. Then you bless them. If you don't, their souls will wander."

❀

May 1945. My mother sat with her grandmother on a stack of adobe bricks behind the ranch house, facing the orchards to the east. Neither spoke. Neither knew what to say.

It had been several days since they buried my mother's aunt Molly, who was run over by a train while saying good-bye to a brother-in-law who had been ordered to the Pacific.

Of the freak accident, the porter said this to a newspaperman: "We were moving out of the station and I was closing the rear door of the second to the last car, when this woman came up and said, 'Wait. I've got to get off.' When I told her, 'You can't get off now, Lady,' she pushed me aside and jumped. She fell or tripped. I don't know what happened."

No one told my mother. No one knew how. Nine months earlier, she had been adopted by Molly after her mother, Desolina, had given birth to a sixth child. At thirty-two, Molly could not have children of her own. She and her husband treated my mother as if she were theirs. They attended Saturday matinees, sampled department store perfume, shared picnics, and jitterbugged to the Andrews Sisters.

Molly was so different from anyone in my mother's family, so generous with kisses, so glamorous with Rita Hayworth curls, so sunny in a yellow silk dress with red roses. My mother missed her parents, loved her parents, but with Molly, in the little yellow house by the tracks, she felt safe.

Ernestina had died the summer before Molly. Maybe her family didn't think my ten-year-old mother could handle the shock. Maybe they were so overcome with their own grief they had forgotten. Whatever the reason, my mother learned of Molly's death only as she knelt before the open casket in church. Bathed in candlelight, rosary in hand, she memorized every detail: the waxy cheek, the putty above the left eyebrow, the gap in the suit sleeve between the right elbow and the right hand, the bouquets of yellow and red roses.

Numb, my mother sat on the earthen bricks as her grandmother sewed a button on pajamas fashioned from Molly's silk dress. My mother gazed across the road at the ripening apples, which glowed gold in the setting sun. In the shade of a crooked limb, she noticed a woman with curly hair, waving.

My mother leaped up and scrambled forward.

"What's wrong?" Adelaida asked. "Where are you going?"

"Auntie Molly!" My mother shouted. "She's there!"

Her grandmother reached for my mother's arm.

"No! Don't go to her."

"But she's here. Under the tree."

Adelaida spun my mother around. Stared into her eyes.

"Molly's gone, mí hijita. Dead."

"No. She's waving to us. See?"

"Listen!" Her grandmother hugged her tight. "I loved your auntie too. And I miss her. I'm sorry I didn't tell you before. But I just couldn't. Molly is gone now. We must let her go. We must pray for her. So her soul won't get lost in purgatory. Do you understand?"

My mother began to cry. When she glanced back at the apple tree, the woman had vanished.

❊

The tin roof of the Guadalupe church flashes before us a quarter-mile to the west between the folds of two slumping hills, a silver buckle on a riding saddle.

"There it is," my mother says, softly. "At last."

I hit the gas, racing the afternoon sun, hoping we can still find the field where Juan Mora died or the adobe where my mother swaddled the stillborn baby, but as the car rumbles toward the Rio Puerco, I notice a cattle gate before us, a padlock and heavy chain, and a No Trespassing sign painted in red letters. On the roadside, a spray of .30-30 shells.

"Oh, I'm sorry," my mother says, touching my forearm. "We've come all this way for nothing."

I shift into park and let the engine idle.

"Not necessarily. We could squeeze through the barbed-wire fence beside the gate. I could hold it open for you."

"No," she says. "They don't like outsiders. Let's go."

"Not yet."

I switch off the engine and hop outside. I try the lock, but it won't budge, so I scramble up a nearby hill for a better look at the church. My mother calls through her window.

"We passed a road a while back that will take us across the river from the west. We could see if it's still there."

I return to the car and wheel around. We find the road, but our path is blocked by an arroyo still glistening from a recent thundershower and slashed deep with 4 x 4 tracks.

"Wait." My mother grabs my wrist. "We'll get stuck."

"We can make it," I say, inching the Honda forward.

"No. Don't risk it. There might be quicksand."

When she was a girl, she explains, Carlos brought her to a crossing like this. The mud was as thick as tar. Although the surface appeared dry, it wasn't, and if you got stuck, you couldn't get out. Her father had seen cattle die that way, frozen in the muck. After he told her that, she never trusted the crossings along the Rio Puerco.

"Just stop here," she says.

I study her puffy eyes and pale skin and decide not to push it. She has taken me as far as she can, or wants to go. And yet, I sense she wants to show me something, or tell me something, so I wait.

Sighing, my mother steps outside and walks among the chamisal and volcanic rock, pausing to study the wind ripples on the dunes. At the arroyo, she kneels to touch the clay.

"Hear that?" she asks, head cocked as I join her.

"What? The wind?"

I stand stock-still, straining to hear it, or feel it, a presence in the land, a current of spirit and memory from which we can draw to fill the spaces within.

Frowning, she wipes her hands and returns to the car.

"Probably just a lost calf."

I watch my mother's silhouette fade into the washboard road, then place my hands on the arroyo bed as she had, palms flat, skin to sand, deep in the moist red earth.

HARDWOOD

1905

My father is born among the oak and pine of eastern Arkansas. As a boy he watches his father guide timber into the steel teeth of the family mill. Wood chips fall like snowflakes. Sawdust stains his skin.

1947

On the rural fringe of northwest Albuquerque, my father buys his first house, Pueblo-style with two bedrooms and one bath. Instead of a den or concrete driveway, he presents the builder with an odd customization—hardwood flooring from his family mill. He supervises the installation himself to ensure each plank is true. When the last hammer falls, he places his palms on the honey-glazed wood and admires the grain.

1971

The ritual begins on Saturdays after Cheerios and *Jonny Quest*. My mother opens the doors and windows and shoos us five kids outside. House to herself, she pours a cup of Lipton tea, places *Abbey Road* on the stereo, and pings open a yellow tin of Johnson Floor Wax. With two fingers she scoops a curl of the sticky brown paste and smooths it onto the floor as gently as face cream. On hands and knees in denim shirt and faded jeans, she rubs with a cotton cloth in tight circles, hour after hour, every inch of every room, as my father instructed before he died. I tiptoe inside to watch her. Dust drifts through the slanting light. The air smells of beeswax. George Harrison sings, "Something in the way she moves."

1990

Twenty-eight years old, away from home for the first time in Southern California, I scan the newspaper to find an apartment for my girlfriend and me. My one requirement: hardwood floors. Although my girlfriend grew up on wall-to-wall carpeting, I insist upon a smooth, hard easy-to-clean surface that reflects the sun. After a month, I find our ideal rental a quarter-mile from the ocean in Laguna Beach: two bedrooms, broad windows, slatted yellow pine floors.

Before we move in, I suggest removing the stain from the maple-colored planks. My girlfriend balks. The job will cost hundreds of dollars. My reply: I'll do it myself.

I rent an industrial belt sander, a handheld edger, and several dozen sheets of multi-grade paper. I strain my back lugging the equipment upstairs, bruise my knees standing on all fours, scrape the skin from my fingers changing the pads, and collect a sawdust paste on my sweaty forehead.

"Give it a rest," my girlfriend says.

"Here's to sandin' with reckless abandon," my friends tease, toasting me with beers.

I kick them out, push down on the edger with all my weight, and feel the motor burn.

1993

After five years away, I visit my mother, swinging back her door to embrace her. The floorboards creak beneath me, as dry gray as the cottonwoods flanking her house.

"What happened?" I say.

My mother squints through a pair of bifocals fastened with a paper clip. "I haven't had time to wax them. With my arthritis, I can't stay on my knees too long."

I run my finger along the rough surface. A sliver snags my skin.

My first home in northwest Denver is fitted with hardwood floors—
thin pine slats installed when the brick bungalow was built in 1926.
The planks aren't as thick as the ones at my mother's. Not as solid.
A vase rattles on a dining room display case when I walk by. My
son's ball thuds on the dead spot in the hall. Nail heads poke from
the water-stained cracks in the bedroom.

"Save your money," a workman tells me. "Aren't worth refinish-
ing. Wood's too soft. Can't take another sanding."

I refinish them anyway, coating the planks with a honey coat of
polyurethane.

Once a day, sometimes twice, I sweep the floors as my mother
taught me, all the corners and crannies. If I notice a stain of apple
juice or Enfamil, I reach beneath the kitchen sink for a cotton cloth
and bottle of hardwood cleaner, then hard rub hard in tight circles.
On hands and knees, leaning close to the glossy surface, I can see
my face.

MONSTER

As a boy, I couldn't sit through an entire episode of *The Munsters*. Whenever the ashen skin and obsidian eyes of the ghoulish family flashed across our TV screen, I bolted. No matter how often my mother assured me that Herman, Eddie, and Grandpa weren't real zombies, werewolves, or vampires, I saw phantoms in every corner. Even the shadows had faces.

One spring morning, my mother returned home from TG&Y with a cure: three cartoonish bubble-bath bottles of Frankenstein, The Wolfman, and The Mummy. Before I could dive under the bed, she sat me down to explain. The green flesh and bloody fangs were only pretend, she said. Like Halloween masks. Look beneath the surface and I'll find only my imagination. As proof, she unscrewed Frankenstein's head and tilted the bottle toward me. It smelled like Juicy Fruit.

The next morning, my big brother tiptoed behind me with The Wolfman bottle and spooked me all over again. Exasperated, our mother hid the plastic bottles in the hall closet beside our father's old ashtray, Civil Air Patrol cap, and Masonic sword. When my brother creaked open the door, I screamed.

※

My teenage uncle, my mother's youngest brother, visited our house on Saturdays to help out with yard work. When he finished, he sat long-haired and barefoot before our black-and-white Zenith for his favorite show, *The Outer Limits*.

When I cringed at the sight of atomic tarantulas and bug-eyed Martians, he pulled me close and whispered a secret: monsters weren't really scary, just misunderstood. The Hunchback, King Kong, and Godzilla were all lonely misfits who attacked only when provoked. Monsters, he said, scratching his whiskers, were mistreated because they were different.

To prove his point, he introduced me to his best friend, a reclusive science whiz with the thick black glasses and brown surfer bangs of Ernie on *My Three Sons*. Alone in his bedroom with the curtains drawn, his friend glued rabbit fur onto a plastic Wolfman model, crafted a black satin cape for The Phantom of the Opera, and wrapped cotton gauze around The Mummy, transforming ugliness into beauty.

My uncle was right, the recluse said, guiding me to a worktable of plastic arms, hands, legs, and heads. Monsters were often noble creatures battling darkness within. Dangerous, yes, but also vulnerable. Remove their masks, look beyond their afflictions, and phantoms were just men. For a second, I thought he was talking about my father's ghost.

Before I left, he gave me a reminder: the webbed hand of The Creature of the Black Lagoon, its scales painted garden-hose green, its claws dripping with red nail-polish blood.

I held it close in the dim light, turning it in my palm like a lucky penny.

❋

Late summer. My brother sauntered home from an illegal fireworks stand one day with a handful of toy creatures he intended to blow up. Spooky Kookys, he called them.

There were six characters in all: a shackled skeleton, two manacled wretches, a shirtless goon, a ragged brute, and a fanged beast in a leafy tunic, each about four inches tall with bulging eyes and wagging tongues. My mother wrinkled her nose at the sight of them. "Disgusting," she said.

These monsters were like nothing I'd ever seen. Unlike my stiff plastic Army men, I could bend the soft rubber Spooky Kookys however I wanted. And with a razor blade and book of matches, I could transplant different heads onto different bodies, different arms and legs onto different torsos, building new men, composite men. From ghouls, I made warriors. From phantoms, princes.

"Why don't you go outside with the other kids," my mother said after I'd played with my monsters for hours on end.

Shrugging, I returned to my netherworld.

One afternoon, I came home from school to find my creatures gone. I checked in my dresser drawers, under my bed, in my pants pockets, in every corner of the house.

"Haven't seen them," my mother said, arms folded. "Maybe they got thrown out with the trash by accident."

I searched for days, weeks, before finally shuffling outside to ride my bike.

Years later, as a grown man, I'd visit my mother's house and catch myself peeking behind chairs or running my hand over the top shelf in the hall closet, hopeful.

RELICS

KEY

I save a key to my mother's door long after I leave home,
but visit only when an EKG bleeps jagged white lines on
a black screen above her hospital bed. She doesn't know
that I've come, that I wander her rooms like one of her
strays, that I linger for hours reading the woman on the
walls. Fingerprints on iron nails. Cursive cracks in sun-
bleached deer bones. Hour after hour in the smoke of
piñon incense.

A red candle flickers beneath a tabletop bust of Jesus
Christ. A black tortoise-shell cat squints from beneath
an empty living room rocker. The key is warm in my fingers. Brown as river clay. Smooth as a penny with the face
rubbed away.

"Keep it," my mother told me. "It's yours."

URN

My mother is five. I see her so clearly in this story she
told, sitting on a bench against the southern wall of her
grandparents' ranch house in Corrales, leaning against
sun-warmed adobe bricks. Her grandfather slouches beside her, repairing a hole in an apple sack. His long curved
needle slips in and out of the burlap as gracefully as a
trout leaping from a mountain stream. Cherry-scented
smoke rises from his pipe into the autumn air to form
a halo around his head of thick white hair. Soothed by
the aroma and the slow rhythm of his work, my mother
breathes deeply, holds it in.

She is not like her sister, brother, or cousins, who hate visiting the ranch while their mothers nurse newborns and their fathers irrigate the alfalfa. They whine when their grandmother hands them baskets to gather breakfast eggs, and cry when their grandfather asks them to churn butter for supper. They'd rather be in school. In the city.

Not my mother. She opens the barn door to a treasure of steel tongs, silver spurs, brass bells, and iron rods. She descends the cellar steps to rows of jewel-colored jars holding cherries, plums, apricots, and honey. At night she dreams to the song of crickets, bullfrogs, coyotes, owls.

"What are you looking at?" her grandfather asks, nudging her with his elbow, breaking her daydream.

She blushes, shifts her weight on the warm adobe bricks.

Her abuelo likes that about her, the shyness. She is always watching, too. Always listening. Always soaking everything in. And she knows the magic of making new from old. When a shirt collar frays, she helps her grandmother cut it away, turn it inside out, and stitch it back into place. When a bridle breaks, she holds the leather strap firm on his workbench while he trims it, attaches a steel buckle, and fits it onto his saddle. One day, he often tells her, she will teach these traditions to her own children.

"Shoot!" The curved needle snaps in his callused fingers. He fishes into the top pocket of his overalls for a spare.

"Can I have it?" my young mother asks.

"What? The needle? Why? You could hurt yourself."

She wrinkles her nose. Her chestnut hair cascades around her shoulders. "I just like it."

Her grandfather chuckles. "Let me file it down first."

He tickles her. She scrunches her neck like a turtle.

That night, my mother pads from bed into the guest-room closet. Kneeling in the moonlight, she unwraps the needle from a handkerchief in her work dress pocket and runs her thumb along the dull tip. Grinning, she reaches beside her boots for her grandfather's cracked wooden tobacco urn. Lifting the lid of the goblet-shaped box, she places the needle among her collection of cobalt beads, wheat-straw pennies, sunflowers, sage roots. Bowl to her nose, she inhales the aroma of smoke, copper, ash, and seeds.

BRANDING IRON

I'm five. I'm supposed to be napping, but I'm not. I'm staring at the branding iron above my big brother's bed. Black. Bumpy. Flecked with orange rust. He and our mother pulled it from the sand while exploring the llano above Corrales. She let him keep it because the tip is shaped into an "R"—like Ray, his name. I'm not allowed to play with it, but I do anyway. While he's at school, I slip the rod from its nail and swing it like a sword, wave it like a wand, and on this afternoon, accidentally bang it against the headboard.

"What are you doing?" My mother stands in the doorway, arms folded.

I flop onto the bed and bury my face in the pillow.

She sits beside me, relic in hand.

"Do you know what this is?" she asks. "When I was little, like you, I used to hang around my grandfather's corral to watch him brand cattle. He used a rod like this one to burn his initials on their behinds. Instead of an 'R,' his branding iron had a 'P'—for Perea, his last name."

I sit upright. "Burn?"

"Oh, yes. He put the branding iron in the campfire until it turned orange. Then he pressed it onto cow's haunches until it burned away the hair and made a P-shaped scar. That way he'd know which cows belonged to whom."

"Did the cows cry?"

She places the rod in my palm.

"A bit. But their skin is thick. Not like ours. But you'd better put it back before your brother brands you!"

I watch her leave, the image of the branding fire glowing as bright in my mind as a tiny sun. I turn the rod in my fingers. Rust flakes onto my skin.

The old Corrales church is closing, the San Ysidro chapel, an adobe rectangle built after the Rio Grande flooded in 1869 and washed coffins as far as Albuquerque. Named after the patron saint of farmers, the poor, and the afflicted, the chapel stands for a century among the apples, chile, and beans before the archdiocese deems it unstable. Doors are bolted shut. Benches, santos, statues, and altarpieces auctioned away.

My mother reads the announcement and tosses aside the evening paper. She was born less than a mile from the church. From the stiff back of the family pew, she watched her grandfather dip his brown hands into the basin bowl of holy water. Helped her grandmother light the candles flickering in the porcelain eyes of Christ. Stood in the llano wind as her baby sister's coffin sank into the camposanto sand.

Desperate for a memento, she phones cousins, farmers, merchants, deacons. But she's too late. Everything's gone.

She searches anyway.

One morning, on her way to visit the river, my mother notices one of the original San Ysidro pews in the backyard of an old woman's roadside home. She knocks on the door and explains her family history, her voice barely a whisper.

Moved by her story, the woman escorts her to the eight-foot bench built in the year of the Little Big Horn battle. My mother cringes to find the pew holding moldy apple crates.

"I'll buy it," she says. "I'll make payments."

My mother digs in her jeans for a five-dollar bill.

"It's all I have."

The woman twists her lips, reads my mother's eyes.

"Take it."

Back home, my mother slides the pew into our living room in place of a couch. She doesn't sand the rough-hewn surface, varnish the dry pine, or even add cushions.

No, she tells me. She wants to feel the grain.

LADDER

Indian summer. My mother rides with her father through the Rio Puerco badlands, his powder blue pickup creaking along the washboard roads. Heat shimmers from the parched earth like reaching silver fingers.

As a young man he traveled this forsaken land, he tells her, mile after mile beneath the Dust Bowl sun. He placed peaches in blistered hands, scattered wheat among cholla, cut furrows from rock, poured water into empty cups.

"Once," he says, reaching a hand out the window to slice the wind, "all this was green."

She soaks in his words as if drawing moisture from air.

In the cracked bricks of a roadside ruin, she notices two poles pointing skyward like antenna. After parking on roadside, she unearths the pine skeleton of a kiva ladder rooted in the red sand. She pitches it into the truck bed.

Once home, she leans the ladder against the sunrise wall of our house. On it she hangs the rings of a produce barrel, a dented water bucket, and a spool of rusted barbed wire.

The ladder is too short to reach the roof, but I climb it anyway. Gazing up, I become dizzy.

HOPE CHEST

One August afternoon my mother gets lost on a cattle trail exploring the hills north of Cuba. She stops at a roadside adobe for directions back to the highway. An old woman invites her inside for a glass of ice water. Beneath the sala window, my mother notices an antique clothing trunk.

"Beautiful," she says, running her fingers along a tarnished nickel surface of butterflies and daisies. "My grandmother had one just like it. Your family must be proud."

The old woman scowls. Once, she explains, the trunk held her dowry of lace, bone china, and silver. Her bridegroom hauled it by buckboard all the way from her family ranch near Colorado. But for decades, it has held only winter blankets.

"My daughters couldn't care less," the old woman says with a wave of her hand. "They think it's old and ugly. But if you like it, go ahead and take it. It's yours."

My mother blushes. "Oh, no. I couldn't accept it for free. But I would like to buy it. How much do you want?"

The woman raises an eyebrow. "How much do you have?"

My mother signs over the fifty-dollar money order that was supposed to pay our light bill.

Back in Albuquerque, she polishes the trunk with steel wool and lemon oil until it shimmers like a treasure chest. Inside she places beaded doeskin moccasins, Yaqui Easter masks, a crown of thorns from the Penitente Brotherhood, a bundle of owl and peacock feathers, Navajo winter blankets, a cracked wooden tobacco urn, my father's ashtray, and a handheld silver mirror, one side convex, the other concave.

ROOT

After college, I trade the range grass and cottonwoods of New Mexico for the bougainvillea and date palms of Southern California, losing myself in tide pools and freeways.

My mother calls on weekend mornings to tell me the land of her childhood—and mine—is dying.

"Developers are destroying this place," she says. "And no one's stopping them. You should come back before it's gone."

I gaze out my window at the sailboats slicing the along the sapphire horizon of Laguna Beach.

"Things change. You can't save the past."

She hangs up mad and mails me boxes of piñon incense and news clippings about a proposed highway through an outcrop of Native American petroglyphs we explored when I was a boy. I read the stories and breathe in the smoke-scented memories.

On a hazy summer afternoon, I hike with friends up a scrubby hill to watch a solar eclipse. Stocked with sunscreen and micro-brewed beer, we smooth our Trotsky goatees and adjust our Melrose shades as the moon slides across the sun, which dims the color of a tarnished penny.

On the way home, I wander off the path seeking odd rocks, rusty wire and dried flowers for my artifact collection. At my feet, I notice a root twisted into a "V." I place it in my palm and flick it. The root spins like a compass needle before stopping. It points behind me, backward, home.

CRUCIFIX

I decorate my new Albuquerque apartment with antiques. My mother beams. As a welcome-home surprise, she buys me a church pew from a secondhand co-op in the Rio Grande farmland. Hand in mine, she leads me through the dim, creaky shop to a back room where she had set aside her own treasure—a handmade wrought iron crucifix edged with roses.

"It's the real thing," she whispers, pinching my arm. "From a church. You can tell by the craftsmanship. By the old Spanish design. I'm going to rescue it."

"Rescue? From who? From what?"

"From the Californians. From the Texans. From the yuppies coming here and bastardizing my land and culture. These things belong in a chapel, or a home, not in a store to be sold for profit. I always thought New Mexico would stay the same. That it would endure. But it hasn't. And it won't. So I'm collecting these things. Saving them."

A sunburned man with a fanny pack narrows his eyes at us, so I nudge my mother toward the front counter. She buys the cross while I load the pew into the back of my pickup. On the way out, I ask the cashier where she assembles her inventory.

"Kansas. Oklahoma." She pops her chewing gum. "We drive out there a few times a year."

"Not from New Mexico?"

"Nope."

That evening, I stand in my mother's dining room while she

removes a calendar of saints to make room for her new antique. I consider telling her what the cashier had said, but change my mind when she hugs my waist and squeezes.

She hands me the hammer. I nail the cross to her wall.

BRANCH

In my column for the evening newspaper, I chase my mother's ghosts. I profile an auto mechanic carving angels from fallen cottonwoods, a retired mailman growing roses de Castilla beside a highway, and a construction worker rebuilding his crumbling adobe church brick by brick.

A century-old cottonwood becomes my symbol, my cause. Gnarled and gray, it stands like a Zuni Shalako in the path of a proposed commuter bridge through the north valley farmland across the Rio Grande to the west mesa suburbs, pitting native against newcomer. While I kneel before the trunk to light candles at a roadside shrine, hate mail collects on my desk.

My mother reads my work and smiles.

The bridge goes through anyway. On a frigid spring morning, city crews bring the cottonwood down. Bulldozers gouge the black soil. Branches bend but hold firm. Shovels snap. Ax handles break. A workman fires a chainsaw.

One year later, I stand at the river's edge with one of the last farmers irrigating the fields. Subarus and Range Rovers crawl across the concrete-and-steel platform painted the colors of New Mexico — adobe, olive, turquoise.

I pluck a dead branch from the thinning grass.

"Can you believe it? They actually built it."

"Yes," the farmer says. "Isn't it beautiful?"

ROSARY

A gray afternoon. Three weeks before Christmas. My mother lies in a hospital bed with chest pains. She's worked herself to exhaustion again, dusting, sweeping, and rearranging her relics for the holidays. She's ignored her doctor's warnings about straining her sixty-year-old heart, forgotten her daily dose of aspirin, and dismissed her regimen of anti-inflammatories. On the way to the emergency room she told paramedics she'd suffered only indigestion. Take her home, she demanded. She would heal at home.

I stand beside her bed cringing at the green tubes in her nose and wrists. It's lunchtime, but she's pushed aside her baked chicken and orange Jell-O. She won't sleep. Won't watch TV. Won't look me in the eye. She hates hospitals with their fluorescent lights, antiseptic smell, and images of her younger sister, her parents, and my father.

"You should eat something," I say, touching her hand.

She gazes out the window at the gravel rooftops and twisted TV antennas. "I'm not hungry."

"Want some juice? Blankets?"

"I want to go home."

I change the subject. "What would you like for Christmas?"

As a boy, I always knew what to get her. A St. Francis of Assisi carving. An owl made of river clay. A strand of cobalt beads. Something to remind her of where she came from and who she was. Always, she placed my discoveries beside her own.

"How about a kachina? A Georgia O'Keeffe print?"

"No," she says, sighing. "I'm through with that. When I leave here, I'm going to rid myself of possessions. Strip my house as bare as a church. Like my grandmother's."

"What about your things? Your relics?"

"We'll see," she says, withdrawing her hand.

I persist. "How about a rosary? I know a woman who owns a botanica near the river. She makes beads from antique silver. They're old. Authentic. New Mexican."

My mother searches my eyes. After a moment, she nods.

MIRROR

Late spring. My mother brings me a gift. I lug it from her car through the sprouting grass and budding cottonwoods of my apartment courtyard. Heavy, awkward, big as a picture window, the bundle nearly slips through my hands.

In the weak light of my front window, I unwrap the protective blankets to reveal an antique mirror with a square wood-block frame, ruddy-brown varnish, beveled edges, and thick glass with the reflective silver flaking away.

"It's very old," my mother says, studying my frown. "Not as ornate as you like, but built to last. The way they made them in my grandmother's day."

I thank her with a hug, then lift the mirror onto the cracked table she gave me after leaving the hospital, placing the frame beside the vase of range grass and bowl of tarnished pennies I've begun collecting. When the mirror slides away, I anchor it to my adobe wall, but it pulls the nails free.

After an hour of jockeying, we hang the bulky frame with baling wire from the ceiling vigas opposite the front door, where my mother says it will give my dark cramped apartment the illusion of light and space.

"Sure you like it?" she asks, touching my arm.

"Of course," I lie.

Once she leaves, I scrub the glass with soap and water, then ammonia and cotton cloth, and still a cloud remains. And yet, if I stand back, if I squint, my reflection is clear.

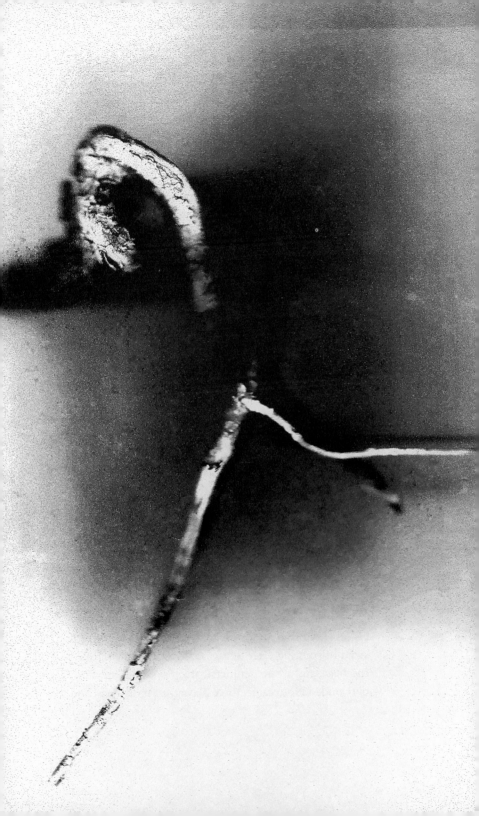

WINDOWS

My mother loved the clear New Mexico sunlight. Each morning she pulled back the curtains to usher in a flood of white. She did not, however, like strangers peering inside our home. Day after day, she adjusted, and readjusted, bamboo shades, rice paper screens, cotton sheets, and Russian olive sticks tacked like wooden bars across the window frames.

Her bedroom, with twelve-paneled windows facing north and east, shone the brightest. At sunrise, her pale walls blazed. Come nightfall, though, the interior stood exposed.

Exasperated, my mother yanked off her curtains one spring morning, uncapped her oil paints, and squeezed a fat curl of violet pigment directly onto the glass. With a palette knife and a wide bristle brush, she smoothed on paint until the front yard pines vanished behind a lavender veil. Next, she chose orange, then red, blue, green, and yellow, one color per panel, until her windows became a Rubik's Cube mural.

No one could see in, but neither could she out. Unfazed, she hung a row of spider ferns from ceiling hooks and pushed her antique brass bed beneath the panes. At daybreak, she woke to the rosy glow of a church.

Inspired by her work, my uncle chose three small panels on either side of our broad living room window. Instead of painting each square a single color, he selected the black-and-white geometric images of a Zuni thundercloud, a Hopi eagle, three Navajo corn maidens, and a Mestizo labyrinth with a black figure lingering at the opening. When the sun rose, his geometric patterns allowed in sharp shafts of light. At dusk, they cast puzzle shadows on the walls.

They saved the most elaborate design for a tall, rectangular panel in our dining room facing the front porch—a portal my siblings and I used to spy on visitors.

With detail brushes and a full palette of oils, my mother and uncle painted a tangerine sun blasting yellow and red rays over a valley of blue saw-toothed mountains and a jade forest of feathery pines. Evening shadows dripped black and purple at the edges of the scene, symbolizing the ageless battle between darkness and light. They left bare glass on only two spots: the eye of the sun and the silhouette of a man on the forest floor standing before a reflecting pool.

I was too short to see through the sun, so when the doorbell rang, I knelt before the solitary figure in the wilderness and peeked out through his empty shape.

MAN IN A BOX

I

A postcard. A faded, wrinkled, colorized street shot of downtown Albuquerque in the rosy afterglow of World War II. "Indian Country," the back caption says. Glossy black sedans crawl like desert beetles along Route 66. The adobe facade of the Franciscan Hotel rises from the dust like an Anasazi ruin. On the south side of the street, between a typewriter shop and a flower stand, hangs a faded green sign with white block letters—Fletcher Drugs, my father's pharmacy.

The image is my family's only record of the landmark. My oldest sister found it in an antique store shoebox while browsing artifacts one afternoon with our mother. I borrowed it, stole it, really, because we're all stingy with his things, because there aren't enough to go around.

Alone at night, forty years after my father's funeral, I study the image like a tarot card. The red Texaco star. The yellow road stripes pointing east. The black silhouette on the sidewalk outside the drugstore—the man in a fedora. I can't make out the face, it's hidden in shadow, but I can see this—he's looking forward, into the camera, at me.

✻

He came to my mother in dreams. He stood at our door with his silver hair and white smock and knocked. Always, she let him in. Then they talked. About her. About us kids.

Often, my father visited in times of change, sickness, crisis. The night before my brother got hit by a car. The night I fell while sleepwalking and suffered a concussion.

We weren't frightened by these dreams. Not really. My siblings and I were more curious than anything. When word filtered down from one of us to the other, we listened.

I'd be sitting at the dining room table eating fried potatoes, tortillas, and green chile for breakfast, when my oldest sister would click shut her compact and face me.

"She dreamed of him again. Dad."

I'd glance into the kitchen at our mother, who'd clatter a teakettle on the gas stove and spark a blossom of blue flame. She'd look over, eyes puffy from sleep, and turn away.

"What did she say?"

"Nothing. Just that she dreamed about him again. But you know what that means, don't you. Be careful."

"I am," I'd say. "I always am."

✸

Seven stories. Of everything my mother shared about my father, seven stories shone brightest. Seven stories she told again and again with folded hands and a breathy voice until her words became my own and my father became myth. Seven stories that stayed with me not only for what they said but for what they didn't say. Seven stories that sparked my desire to know him, touch him, invent him.

I.

My father, Ray, adored his father, Charles, a bear-like man who could drink an entire quart of whiskey and still walk straight. Handsome, charming, and affectionate, with a shared love of pranks and boxing, no one in their family could hold a grudge against Ray or Charles. No matter how often they belched during Bertha's Sunday dinner, or surprised Daisy in her schoolgirl bloomers, or wrestled bookish Harrison to the floor, once they grinned their impish grins, all was forgiven.

On mornings when Charles left for weeks at a time as a locomotive engineer, my father watched from the window as the broad-shouldered silhouette faded into the shadows. When Charles finally lumbered up the cobblestone walkway with his duffel bag, my father scrambled out for their welcome-home ritual: removing the big man's soot-stained clothes. Charles plopped onto the porch step and extended his limbs while my father, as reverently as a page peeling away knight's armor, removed boots, bib, coveralls, and flannel shirt, everything but long johns. Task complete, man and boy locked arms and sauntered inside, inseparable.

2.

While Charles rode the rails, my father often slipped by his grammar school truant officer to roam the factories, rail yards, and river docks of Des Moines, seeking comfort in the wide shoulders and thick necks he watched from afar.

One afternoon he followed a plume of smoke on the horizon, walking until the cobblestones gave way to mud, toward an open field where one locomotive had crashed into another, the second toppled onto its side.

He stepped into the meadow as if entering a dream, passing objects scattered throughout the waist-high grass—a parasol, a rag doll, a violin, a top hat. Among the twisted steel and broken wood, he noticed at his feet something pale white, delicate as bone. He picked it up.

At that moment, he saw a white flash, smelled a whiff of sulfur, and wheeled around to face a man kneeling beneath the black hood of a tripod camera.

My father blinked, ran.

3.

His mother, Bertha, was afflicted with a weak heart. She could barely cross a room without pausing for breath.

One morning, with her children in school and her husband asleep, she settled in her parlor with tea and a newspaper. Sipping her hot chamomile, she scanned the headlines, then dropped the cup, and swooned. There, in a front-page photo of a train crash, stood the ghostly image of her young son, my father, staring at her from the frame.

Then this: a few days later, after Charles placed my father under the truant officer's thumb, Bertha sat in her kitchen washing the soot from the boy's knickers when she felt a cigar-like object in his pocket. Worried that he'd begun smoking, she fished out the cylinder, held it to her nose, then staggered away for her smelling salts.

My wayward father had kept a souvenir from the train crash: a dead man's finger, severed at the knuckle.

4.

December 1918. Charles returned from work from usual, sat on the step, and offered his boots to my father, who frowned at the engineer's slow movements and clammy skin.

The Spanish flu had ravaged Des Moines. Schools closed. The mayor ordered masks in public. Despite the end of World War I and the coming holidays, streets emptied.

Breathing heavily, Charles set aside his soiled clothes and shuffled inside, hardly glancing at his wife and children before climbing the stairs to his bedroom.

At the top step, Charles gripped the rail, turned slightly to his left, and tumbled back down, dead from a massive heart attack before he hit the floor. My father, three weeks from his thirteenth birthday, saw it all.

5.

Summers in Edina, Missouri. So much green. My father, removed from the grays and browns of Des Moines, and the flashes of Charles at the bottom of the stairs, spent summers there with Bertha's family, at Bertha's insistence, to heal. For a time, with the gazebos and fireflies, with his cousins, Rex, Ed and Jimmy, with the hugs from a black housekeeper, and the talks with her fatherless son, he did.

But one evening on the way to town, he passed a roadside tree where a black man hung from a rope and a leering crowd gathered like flies. In the dead man's face, he saw his housekeeper, her son, and Charles. My father ran toward the horizon, ran to forget.

6.

They were opposites, the two brothers, as different as night and day. Like their father and his father. Like all Fletcher men. Where Ray was gregarious, emotional, and generous, Harrison was aloof, cerebral, and thrifty. After Charles died, Harrison, older by three years, quit high school to support the family as a telegraph clerk, abandoning college aspirations to save every dime. My father, who yawned over books, was allowed to continue his studies, working part-time at a drugstore soda fountain and blowing money on clothes.

One evening, my teenage father returned home to find Harrison modeling his favorite silk shirt.

Take it off, Ray said. The garment was his.

Harrison adjusted the cufflinks, grinned.

My father swung first, and the brothers fought, breaking chairs and tables before Bertha appeared in the doorway, hand to her chest. Harrison ripped off the garment and left.

Later, he explained to Bertha why he had borrowed my father's favorite shirt without permission: he had proposed to his high school sweetheart and wanted to celebrate.

My father apologized, but the damage was done. Harrison married and moved across town, away from his family, away from my father.

7.

Summer, 1932. Bertha, bedridden again, asked my father to make a promise: find her nephews, Rex, Ed, and Jimmy, who'd run away from their Missouri home years earlier after the death of Bertha's younger sister. The boys, fleeing the beatings of a stepmother, had hopped a freight car west. Bertha, weighed by guilt, had vowed to watch over them.

My father, determined to make things right, hired Pinkerton detectives, who eventually tracked the cousins to Albuquerque, where Rex owned a shoe shop and Jimmy worked as an auto mechanic. Ed, meanwhile, had moved on to San Francisco to play concert piano.

Burden lifted, Bertha lived another ten years before her heart finally failed.

My father would not remain at her side. Promise fulfilled, fresh from pharmacy school at age twenty-seven, he boarded a passenger train south by southwest to follow his cousins, never to return.

❀

I have one memory of my father. I'm straddling a knee. I know it's not my mother's knee because she's standing in front of me turning the knobs on our black-and-white TV. I'm playing with a toy, maybe it's a puppet, and it falls to the hardwood floor with a clack. I slide off this knee to retrieve my plaything, and a gentle hand guides me down.

I toddle away, toward the flickering light.

❀

My father collected guns. Vintage pistols. Before entering the hospital, he sold all but one—a Peacekeeper, I think it was, which my mother hid in the hall closet.

One afternoon while we were supposed to be napping, my brother and I slipped from our room to find it. "I'm the man of the house," he whispered. "The gun's mine."

Standing on his toes, he ran his fingers along dark cardboard shapes until he settled on a small wooden rectangle at the back of the bottom shelf. Holding his breath, he brought down the container, creaked it open, and angled a shiny blue barrel of the Colt revolver toward the light filtering in from the living room window. As I reached for it, our mother swung the door open wide.

The pistol wasn't loaded, but she wouldn't stop crying.

The next day, with my brother in school, my mother and I drove to Doc Holiday's pawnshop. I remembered the name, the outlaw name, and the bars on the windows.

I pushed open the door. A silver bell tinkled. Two men behind the counter stopped talking and looked at us. The tall one elbowed the short one and they smiled. They always smiled. The mailman. The gas station mechanic.

My mother squeezed my hand.

At the register, she squared her shoulders, set the wooden box on the counter, and opened it. The tall one stroked his beard. The short one whistled through his teeth. While they talked, I stared at the long glass cases of man things—pocketknives, hunting knives, and fishing knives, handles wrapped with leather, handles carved from antlers, handles made of bone, blades bright as mirrors.

On the way home, the empty box beside her, my mother dabbed tissue under her Jackie O sunglasses. I stood on the hump in the backseat and touched her shoulder.

"Don't worry. I'll protect you."

She glanced in the rearview and tried to smile. In the black ovals of her eyes, I saw myself.

✻

I inherited the sword. Before my father died, he decided that I, not my brother, would receive the ceremonial blade from the Masonic Order, to which his family belonged.

I was proud of my heirloom. I sneaked into the hall closet to play with it while my mother pruned roses outside. I slipped the dull weapon from its tarnished brass sheath, gripped the chipped black wooden handle with the knight's helmet hilt, and ran my finger along the chrome surface etched with vines and writing I couldn't read.

My brother slid beside me into the cool darkness.

"It's not real," he said, poking my ribs. "Mom told me the old Masons used to tap the young Masons on the shoulder when they joined the club. It's only for show."

I didn't believe him. Didn't want to believe him. I wanted to believe our father had chosen me as the family guardian, the protector. To prove it, I challenged our little sister to a duel while our mother weeded her irises.

As her weapon, my sister selected our mother's Russian olive switch. We battled up and down the hallway. She drove me back with every blow—rattling my foil so hard it hurt. When she swirled her stick like a musketeer, I jabbed her knuckle.

I apologized, but she told anyway, and our mother packed away my heirloom until I was "old enough to deserve it."

My brother laughed, but I didn't mind.

My sword drew blood.

✻

A letter arrives at my newsroom desk. A white envelope with the afternoon mail, my name written across the front in a blue ballpoint cursive I don't recognize.

I rip open the edge and unfold a clean typewritten note. It's from a woman who worked at my father's drugstore in the early fifties before he met my mother. A woman who recognized my byline and brooding eyes in my column mug. A woman, Dorothy Lawson, who tells me things about my father I never knew.

His second wife: "She was German and wore her hair in braids. After she died, he was very lonely. They were never able to have children. He used to tell me how much he wanted children, but it didn't seem that he was meant to have any. The pharmacy became his life."

His habits: "He'd bring his cigarettes and sit at the soda fountain and watch me work. He'd sit there and laugh at my childish impatience. I should have been fired lots of time, but he never got mad. He was always patient and kind, watching me with his sad eyes, smiling quietly."

How he met my mother: "I remember the day when she came to work in our store. She was so very beautiful and serene. So very different from anyone I knew. His step had quickness to it. He smiled brightly. He spent more and more time talking with her. Long, quiet conversations punctuated by his gentle chuckles and her shy laugh."

How he died: "After I married, I saw in the paper your father had passed. I called your mother and she said he went in for an eye exam and the doctor saw a tumor."

Reading the note, I feel a presence, as if someone is watching me. When I look around, the reporter in the next cube clatters on her keyboards, head down, and at the city desk, empty chairs. Smoothing the crisp paper, I read again, lips moving silently under the pale wash of fluorescent lights.

✻

I show my mother the letter. Read it to her. Visit her house one evening after work hoping we can talk. Arms folded, she leans against the kitchen counter, studying the floor.

"Yes, I remember Dorothy. She was a little dingbat. She doesn't know what she's talking about."

When I continue reading, her lips tighten.

"I've already told you this. You just don't remember."

When I persist, she wipes her hands on her denim housedress, shakes her head, and turns her back.

"I have to make supper."

I try again a few days later with even less success. Leaving the kitchen, I settle on the front porch step to cool down. Inside, cabinets bang and slam. My oldest sister, our mother's confidante, sits beside me, flicks a lighter, and takes a long drag from a thin brown cigarette.

"Mom doesn't understand why you're doing this," she says. "No one does. She thinks you're trying to get back at her for something, or blaming her for something, and using Dad as an excuse. I think you're having a mid-life crisis."

Turning from her, I want to say, what's to understand? He was our father. I want to know who he was. Why we don't speak his name. Why his absence draws me toward it. Why I can't shake the feeling he's in some kind of purgatory, lost and forgotten. But I don't say anything. I don't know how.

My sister flicks away her cigarette ash.

Smoke drifts into the dusky sky.

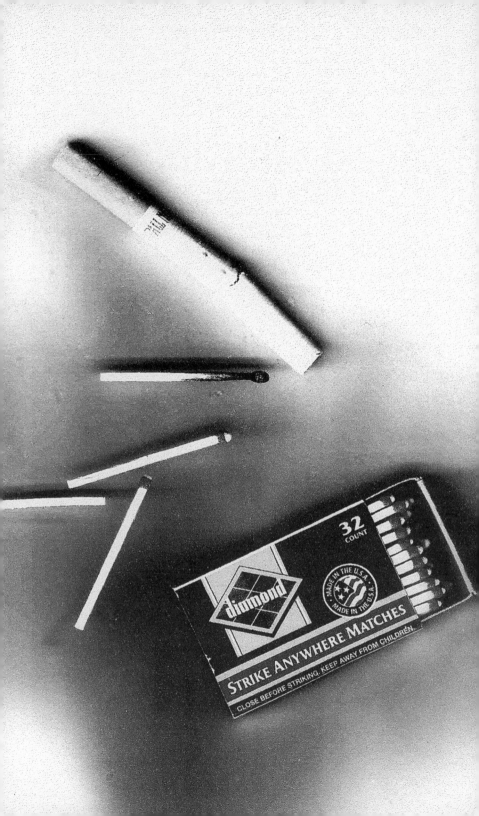

II

I cross the water in a dream, step by step over the wooden footbridge of an acequia near the Rio Grande. The current is glassy green. The cottonwoods sunrise orange.

Spreading my arms to my keep balance, I glance at the opposite ditch bank to gauge my progress and he is there, my father, wearing a black overcoat, black trousers, and shiny black shoes. His thick dark hair is slicked back. His skin alabaster. He watches me through obsidian eyes.

I stop and steady myself, uncertain why he has come to me, since he never has before. Face blank, my father raises his right hand and gazes up at the canopy of branches. I follow his line of sight, but can't see what he wants me to see. Something rustles, maybe an owl.

When I turn to face him, my father nods as if to say, "keep looking," so I tilt my head back until I'm dizzy, until I feel a release, a sensation of working tangles from a woman's wet hair.

❋

Hunter, Arkansas. My father's birthplace. I arrive in the rain, in late autumn, driving a purple Geo rental through Ford Country, wearing a black leather jacket among men in camouflage. I come for a weekend with little more than a map, a notebook, my mother's stories, and a string of facts: my father was born here on Christmas Eve 1905, the youngest of three children; his father ran a sawmill here before becoming a railroad engineer in Des Moines; his grandfather made a fortune selling lumber in Arkansas, Iowa, and Missouri.

I have this, too: my name. I'm the third in my family to bear it, after my great-grandfather and uncle. It's the one clue my father did leave, the one invitation into his past.

When my mother was pregnant with my brother, she and my father made a deal: she'd name the girls, he'd name the boys. While she chose names inspired by books and films, he favored the traditional: his name for my brother, Harrison for me.

"If the children ever want to know about me or my family," he told my mother, "tell them to follow the name."

So far, it has led me here, twelve hundred miles from home to a dot on the map between Little Rock and Memphis, a scattering of A-frames, rust-stained warehouses and a dented sign leaning from the roadside weeds, "Pop. 136." It has also led to Howard Brenniman, the oldest man in fifty miles, a gas station attendant told me, and the keeper of town history.

When I knock on his farmhouse door, Brenniman listens to my explanation, raises his white bushy eyebrows, and ushers me inside. While I settle on his lumpy couch, he flops into an easy chair, flicks a silver lighter, and sparks a tiny black pipe. "Rock of Ages" blares from the kitchen. The aroma of boiled carrots and broccoli wafts through the air. Plastic cups, pipe cleaners, newspapers, and empty Campbell's soup cans clutter every table and shelf in the room.

"What did you say your daddy's name was again?" Brenniman asks after a while, sinking into the black cushions.

When I tell him, he squints through a blossom of cherry-scented smoke, leans into the long brown shadows, and begins at the beginning. Born in 1908, he spent his entire life in Hunter with a younger brother, a few uncles, and modest farm and market. He was married once, for a week, before moving home with his family, who died off in the seventies. Now it's just him, seven chickens, two goats, and a black-and-white TV.

"Doing good just to fix myself a meal," he says, his words bubbling up through a pair of baggy lips.

I study his dark eyes and flaccid skin and realize, had my father lived, he would be about the same age. He and Brenniman might have attended the same schools, paddled the same swimming holes, walked the same woods, and fished the same streams. But when I ask him, the old man doesn't recall.

"Wish I could help more," he says through a sigh. "Your daddy's family might have up and left. Like the rest."

When Brenniman details the slow decline of Hunter, I close my notebook and jingle my keys. Sensing my impatience, he snuffs his pipe and shuffles into a back room to retrieve a black-and-white photo of several dozen children standing before a white clapboard church or a school, frowning into the sun in ruffled dresses, knickers, and button-down shirts.

"I don't know any of them kids," he says, sparking his pipe again, and disappearing behind a cloud of smoke. "It was taken when I was little. You go ahead and hold onto it as long you need to. Your daddy could be there, I suppose."

I pass my fingers over the image as if reading Braille, seeking the brooding gaze or uneasy smile from the snapshots in my mother's hall closet, but recognize none. My father could be among these children and I will never know.

On the way out of town, I park beside the cracked "Welcome to Hunter" sign for a last look around. Stepping onto the roadside, a semi slams through a pothole and drenches me with rainwater. I drop my keys. Cursing, I kneel in the grass to retrieve them and notice a scrap of faded paper at my feet. I pick it up, wipe it off, and unfold a hundred-dollar bill.

I feel a presence again, but when I look around, I'm alone. Scanning the matted grass and gravel, I find no wallet, purse, envelope, or other bills.

It's my father, I tell myself. I feel him. He's saying, "Keep looking."

❋

One summer night, I stayed up late with my brother and sisters to watch a monster movie. We unfolded the living room davenport, flicked off the lamps, and sat in our flannel pajamas munching popcorn. As the opening credits rolled, a name flashed across the black-and-white screen—Ray Fletcher.

"That's dad's name!" my middle sister screamed.

The davenport began to shake. The lamp chain tinkled against the darkened bulb.

"It's his ghost," my big sister whispered, teeth chattering, and the four of them ran into our mother's room.

From down the hall, I heard our mother say, "It's just a tremor," but I could tell from her voice she was listening.

I stayed in the living room, bathed in flickering light.

*

Des Moines, Iowa. My father's hometown. I arrive in the rain. In the winter. The sky bleeding purple and black over a horizon of bare branches, brick chimneys, and utility wires.

I spend the morning in the historical library scouring documents as brittle as fallen leaves. City directories. Census listings. News archives. Cemetery records. School rosters. Hour upon hour under the hum of florescent lights. I learn things. Things about my father's family. Things my mother never knew. Where they lived, worked, when they died.

My father left Hunter for Des Moines in 1909, at age four, when his father, Charles, took an engineer's job at the Rock Island Railroad. The family moved five more times in nine years before settling on the city's east side between the golden capitol dome and gray wall of a flour mill. In December 1918, Charles died at forty-four. My father's siblings, Daisy and Harrison, quit school to support the family, she as a stenographer, he as railroad messenger boy. My grandmother Bertha remained a widow five years before marrying a neighborhood grocer, John Winegar. My father stayed in school while his siblings worked, graduating at age twenty.

In the 1926 East High yearbook, his black hair is parted in the middle, his bowtie knotted against a crisp white collar, and his suit jacket tailored around his broad shoulders. His dark eyes smolder like Rudolph Valentino's. The caption reads, "Who is it can read a woman?"

Turning these pages, my pulse quickens, as if I'm solving a mystery. When I discover in the yearbook the photograph of my father's first wife, Elnor Peterson, I feel as though I'm being guided through the past, as if I'm meant to be doing this.

In Elnor's portrait, her dark pageboy perfectly frames her round face, a twin of Mary Pickford. Her caption reads, "Pretty to walk with, witty to talk with, as charming a girl as you'd ever meet." I imagine my dashing young father sweeping her off her feet. Who can read a woman, indeed.

But as quickly as the excitement rose, it turns to frustration. The more I discover, the more I want to know. I can learn only so much from names, dates, addresses, captions, and job titles. Like my mother's stories, the yearbook photos only whet my appetite.

My family, for instance, has only one image of my grandparents Charles and Bertha—two black-and-white cameos of him in a gray suit, bull-necked and narrow-eyed, and her in a lace collar with thick eyelashes and dark hair. Neither smiles. I don't know when the images were taken, or why.

Stomach tight, I leave the library and drive east across the Des Moines River to the weedy lots, taquerias, and railroad tracks of my father's old neighborhood. Standing outside the squat brick bungalow where he once lived, I scan the walls and windows for fingerprints, faces, but the shades are drawn, the driveway is empty, and the footpath is choked with crabgrass. I knock, but no one answers. In the distance, I hear the groan of machinery, the clang of metal on metal.

By evening, cold and tired, I arrive at the cemetery on the southeast edge of town, wandering nearly an hour before literally stumbling upon three pink marble headstones in the sunken grass—Charles, Bertha, and a two-year-old I don't know, Betty Jean. The markers are small, crowded, bearing no decorations or epitaphs. A dozen rows over, I glance up and into the black monument of Daisy and her husband, Ernie Swanson. Harrison, I've learned from records, lies across town with his wife's family, apart from his parents and sister.

The wind cuts through my jacket. A crow slices through the evening sky. Looking at these relatives, these strangers, I don't know whether to be mad at my mother, my father, or myself. I'd come all this way hoping to stir warmth or sorrow or any feeling at all connecting me to this kin, but I bring no flowers to these graves, and leave nothing behind.

❋

As a boy, while I was supposed to be napping, I'd sneak into the hall closet, stand on my toes, and slide from the shelf a cardboard box of snapshots. Crowded by wool coats and scuffed boots, I'd sit on the floor sifting through Polaroids for a faded eight-by-ten black-and-white of my father.

It was a simple pose, a head-and-shoulders shot for a résumé or a passport, a moment of possibility and promise. His black hair is slicked back. His lips smile slightly, as if amused by his viewer. Facing right, dark eyes shining, he wears a black suit, black tie, and crisp white shirt.

In the pale light, I'd hold the image close, my father as I'd always wanted to see him—young, healthy, immortal.

※

Ottumwa, Iowa. More rain. More gray. After visiting my father's hometown, I visit my great-grandfather's. I drive by the steel skeleton of the Des Moines River bridge, the smog-stained statue of an Indian chief, and the grimy bricks of a meatpacking plant, groggy from a cold, crossing off addresses with a black pen. After only two hours, I'm ready to leave.

I find the site of the Fletcher Lumber Company, where my great-grandfather had made his fortune, only to discover that it has been replaced by a padlocked GO-Tane gas station. I park outside the gray A-frame the patriarch built for his family, but find it as silent as my father's bungalow in Des Moines. Convinced this trail is as cold as the others, I arrive at my final destination—another grave, a black marker that makes me shudder: "Harrison Fletcher January 1850–July 1930." Staring at my name, I feel as if I've been visited by the ghost of Christmas past, examining the path of difficult life for clues how to correct the future. The names beside my great-grandfather's only heighten the sense of disorientation—"Catherine August 1854–March 1894. Icle Dec. 22, 1890, April 17, 1899." More relatives. More strangers.

Wiping mist from the marble, I notice that my great-grandfather's monument is the largest in its row—four feet tall, mounted on a granite slab, decorated with grapevines—a perfect match to the personality my mother had described. In fact, standing beside his grave, the scattered anecdotes begin to coalesce, and I realize how much my mother did share with me, how much I might actually know.

The patriarch, she said, was arrogant, stubborn, and hard drinking. At eleven, he ran away from home after his mother died, fleeing the beatings of his father's new bride. At fourteen, he joined the Union army during the Civil War, sitting out one battle after another in an infirmary bed with mumps or bronchitis before returning unscathed to Iowa, where he became wealthy selling lumber during Reconstruction.

Although he lavished himself with luxury—renting entire hotel floors on business trips and hiring a woman chauffeur—he vowed to spend all his money before he died so his twelve children would have to work as hard as he did. When his wife died first, he married her younger sister within months, opening a lifelong rift with his oldest son, my grandfather, Charles, who grieved his mother by shoveling coal into the churning engine of a locomotive. Ironically, Charles would behave just as callously as his father, abandoning his first wife and two young sons to marry my grandmother Bertha, a raven-haired beauty he met while passing through Missouri. After Charles died, the lumber magnate refused to help my father's struggling family in any way, offering condolences but nothing more, opening another lifelong wound.

Kneeling on the matted yellow grass, I stare down at the twisted roots of my father's family legacy—three generations of grieving sons trying to fill the space of a lost parent with wealth, whiskey, women, cigarettes, and miles and miles of open road, forever leaving one family in search of another.

I place my camera on a nearby headstone, compelled in some strange way to mark this moment, and set the timer. I don't smile or look into the lens, but turn away to avoid the flash. When the strobe pops, I face my great-grandfather's memorial while my eyes adjust. For a moment, I see only a white blossom swallowed by wet black stone.

Before returning to my hotel, I check the county archives to cross the last address from my list. On a grainy spool of microfilm, I discover a divorce deposition filed in June 23, 1932, by Elnor Peterson, my father's first wife.

I steady my pen, and begin to write.

The couple married on February 3, 1929, in Nevada City, Iowa. He was twenty-three and she was twenty-one. They lived in downtown Des Moines, where he clerked at a pharmacy and she took a stenographer's job. After three years, they separated.

Peterson accused my father of "cruel and inhuman treatment" that left her "sick and nervous practically all the time." And while she'd been a "loving and dutiful wife" who worked at the marriage and contributed financially, my father stayed out drinking all night, returning home with threats of striking her—actually did strike her. Edna Fatland, Peterson's friend, witnessed it, and testified.

My father didn't contradict the accusation. Didn't attend the hearing. He'd already left for Albuquerque, Peterson told the judge. The divorce was finalized on July 22, 1932.

The words flicker on the screen, white on black, burning the veneer from my lifelong image of my father. My mother always described him as even-tempered, gentle, and generous. She said he was allergic to alcohol and never touched a drop. She said he came to New Mexico seeking long-lost cousins, not fleeing a broken marriage. Although I know there's another side to the deposition, I can't square in my mind the notion of my father as an accused drunk and wife-beater.

I walk to the restroom, splash cold water on my face, and return to my cubicle. The deposition doesn't read easier the second time. I'm sickened at the notion of my father hitting his wife, yet, for the first time, I see him as a man, not a myth—wounded, flawed, running.

*

My mother won't speak to me. Won't return my calls. A week after returning from Arkansas and Iowa, I hear from my sisters she doesn't like my rummaging through her past and stirring old ghosts. My explanations don't seem to help.

One morning, my mother phones me at work. "Listen," she says, and the torrent comes. She tells me everything she knows about my father. What he said. What she remembers. She rants. Cries. Talks until her phone dies. When it's over, I hold the receiver to my ear, her words echoing above the static.

"Your father was a private man. He never talked much about his personal life."

"Your father had nothing in common with his family. He left Iowa and never returned. They were all dead by the time we met."

"His brother got all the family heirlooms because he was the older son. That's why there's nothing for you kids."

"Your brother couldn't accept your father's death. I did what the child psychologist told me to do—change his surroundings, take down your father's things, make your brother understand your father wasn't coming back."

"You never asked, so I thought you never wanted to know."

And there they were—the answers I've always wanted. For years I've interpreted my mother's silence as her way of keeping my father's memory to herself, but now I can see it perhaps for what it was—a private grief, a way of holding herself together while raising five small children, a means of survival. She and my father had been together only seven years. She was very young. In that time they had five children. Maybe she didn't know him well. Maybe he didn't tell her everything about himself. Maybe she knew all she needed to know. Maybe she really has told me everything, but I've focused so intently on what I didn't know that I've overlooked what I did.

My mother didn't drink. Didn't run to another man. She did what the psychologist told her to do. Maybe she thought the silence would protect us. Maybe she thought time would heal our wounds. Maybe she intended to bring him into our lives but, as the years passed, found herself moving on. Maybe the secrecy around my father was all a sad misunderstanding.

Or maybe, in the end, there just wasn't much to say.

III

A shadow man stands on the ditch bank holding a leather book beneath his left arm. Beside him sits a boy, me as a toddler with Beatle bangs and Keds. As I approach, the man hands the boy the heavy volume. Sitting crossed-legged in the dirt, the boy turns the pages, and the shadow man scribbles in a notebook. When the boy raises his hand with a question, the shadow man bends down to explain, nodding, writing notes.

All at once they stop and look at me, waiting for me to join them, to look inside the dark volume, but I back away, unsure I want to read the words, what they might say, that I shouldn't be here, that I must stop searching.

❋

I assemble my father. Bit by bit a composite forms.

He arrived in Albuquerque in the summer of 1932 at the height of the Great Depression, leaving a broken marriage and drinking problem to join his two wayward cousins from Missouri. He rented a flat at the downtown Elk's Club, took a job at a small downtown drugstore, and began again.

Within a year, my father made a reputation for himself by hand-delivering prescriptions to mechanics and mayors alike, charming even Al Capone, my mother said, while the gangster hid from the Feds in the Jemez Mountains. My father's secret—with each parcel, he included a box of bonbons.

He also charmed a woman, Hede Rosenberg, a tall, pretty, twenty-four-year-old brunette who had fled Hitler's Germany a year earlier with her family. She worked as a hat clerk a few blocks from his pharmacy. They passed each other on the sidewalk, smiled over cups of coffee at the corner diner, or met over the counters of their respective workplaces.

The attraction, it seemed, was immediate. In her, a woman who had left her birthplace and family roots, perhaps my father saw a yearning for a home. In him, a man who carried the weight of his past, perhaps she saw a loss she recognized.

Whatever the bond, they married before a justice of the peace in August 1933, a year after he arrived. Rex Sinnock, one of my father's long-lost cousins, served as best man.

Six years into his new life, my father opened his own pharmacy downtown on the western end of the Route 66 business loop. With Hede at the register and him in the back, he worked six days a week mixing cough syrups, hand-rolling pills, and perfecting the recipe of cherry Coke, carving a niche among his competition. Where Sun Drugs advertised "Russell Candies," Highland Pharmacy sold "Ladies Air-Maid Hosiery," and King Drugs offered "Steaks and Chicken," my father kept it midwestern simple with "Prompt Free Delivery Service."

One summer day, a photographer hopped onto the Route 66 traffic median to snap a postcard of downtown Albuquerque, capturing forever the green-and-white Fletcher Drugs sign.

In February 1943 my father joined the Army. Driven perhaps by memories of the Armistice Day March in Des Moines twenty-five years earlier, or a teenage stint with the Iowa Volunteer Cavalry, or appeals from his Jewish wife, he declined his pharmacist's deferment and enlisted.

At thirty-seven, a heavy smoker, my father scrambled through boot camp beside men half his age. After graduation, he stood for a photo in the courtyard of his Idaho base. Hands at his sides, uniform pleated, he beamed in the noon sun. The man who left Iowa under a cloud of disappointment had become a businessman, devoted husband, and wartime staff sergeant running the base pharmacy. The black sheep had made good.

He was stationed at the Presidio in San Francisco, the nerve center for the Allied Western defense. Beneath the red-tile roofs of the Lincoln Hospital, he worked day and night treating the tens of thousands of wounded soldiers pouring in from the Pacific. He not only dispensed medicine, but administered anesthesia while surgeons fitted pins and plates to broken bodies. In the faces of the dying men, perhaps he saw his father on the stairway landing, or his mother in her sickbed, or the black man hanging from the tree.

Perhaps these visions pushed him to work harder than he should have, longer than he should have, trying to heal himself as much as them.

At the Presidio he suffered his first heart attack, collapsing on tile floor, cigarette sailing away, slipping toward unconsciousness gazing at the white ceiling bulbs.

❋

When peacetime arrived, my father bought his first home—a modest two-bedroom, one-bath, one-car garage, Pueblo-style bungalow among the cottonwoods and acequias of Albuquerque's north valley. He sold his drugstore, resumed management of another pharmacy across from the public library on Route 66, and joined the Civil Air Patrol, making captain. Recovering from his heart attack, he sought comfort in the familiar—growing dahlias like his mother, Bertha, who died during the war, breeding Boston terriers like his sister, Daisy, and corresponding with his brother, Harrison, who shared his damaged heart. At forty-two, perhaps he spoke of children.

Then death came. In November 1951, Harrison reclined on his Des Moines couch for an after-dinner nap and suffered a massive heart attack. He was forty-eight. My father, weakened from angina, could not attend the funeral. Sixteen months later, Daisy woke in the middle of the night, shuffled into her Des Moines kitchen for a glass of water, and collapsed from a cardiac arrest before taking a sip. A heavy smoker, she was fifty-three. In 1957, Hede succumbed to ovarian cancer.

Childless, widowed, the last member of his family, my father lost himself in his work. Day after day, he sat at the back counter of his pharmacy soda fountain with his pack of Pall Malls and cup of black coffee, surrounded by smoke.

❋

When my parents met in the spring of 1957, my father dabbled in photography. He developed his own film, enlarged his own prints, and mixed his own colors. My mother, it seemed, was his favorite model. He snapped shot after shot of her with her head thrown back like Marilyn Monroe, or her eyes smoldering like Grace Kelly. Through the lens of his Speed Graphic, she was flirtatious, open, vulnerable.

In his largest portrait, an eighteen-by-twenty-four, she stands with her back against a white wall wearing an earth brown dress and a heavy gold chain. Half smiling, chestnut hair flowing, she looks up as if pondering a question, or watching the fading curl of my father's cigarette smoke. Her cheeks are flushed, her lips cherry red, brighter than life, as he saw her, as he made her. In the lower right corner, he left his name, Ray A. Fletcher, stamped into the fiber.

❄

August 1996. My grandmother, my mother's mother, was dying. Her kidneys had failed. Her belly had swelled to the size of a watermelon. Under doctor's orders, but against her wishes, she had entered hospice. My family kept a vigil in shifts—door closed, shades drawn, swamp cooler rattling on the windowsill. My grandmother slept hard, her forehead beaded with sweat, her dry lips ringed with spittle. On the pillow beside her head rested a brass crucifix and two white candles.

It was my first adult experience with death. I shuttled aunts to and from the airport, fetched pizza, entertained nieces and nephews. When my mother entered the room, eyes swollen from crying, jaw set hard, I couldn't meet her gaze.

"Make sure someone is always here," she said to everyone and no one. "She doesn't want to be alone."

My grandmother, like my mother, dreamed of spirits, but pushed them away for fear they'd claim her. At eighty-five, after a life of prayer and penance, it seemed to me, they were coming.

After midnight on the third day, I broke from the sickroom to rest. An aunt from California, a holistic healer, leaned beside me in the hallway, caressing a purple medicine pouch. She and my mother, her older sister, had once been close, but had drifted apart for reasons I never knew.

"I feel his presence," my aunt said. "Your father's."

Suddenly awake, I glanced down the darkened corridor.

"You do?"

"Yes. He died beautifully, you know. He turned on his side and just . . . went."

I folded my arms.

"Really?"

She studied my face, considering what she might say next, then smiled, touched my shoulder, and shuffled down the hall.

Later that morning, I cornered my mother in the kitchenette to relay what my aunt had said. My mother, eyes narrowed, tossed her teabag into the trash and walked away.

"How would she know? She wasn't there."

❋

On hands and knees I fumble through my apartment closet for the files I had gathered in Hunter, Des Moines, and Ottumwa, seeking notes I might have overlooked, details that might fill in the gaps to what my mother had told me over the phone at work. In a briefcase buried under basketball shoes and sweatshirts, I discover a folder labeled "Dad." Inside, I find a letter with the heading "FINAL SUM-MARY—Death."

I pull the string on the overhead bulb. I know this letter. It's part of my mother's application for VA survivor's benefits, the official record of my father's final hospital stay. I had requested it before visiting Arkansas and Iowa, when I had cast a wide net for any and all documents bearing his name. I had set it aside in the rush to prepare for my trip and promptly forgotten. Or maybe I wasn't ready to know what it said. Leaning against the doorframe, I begin to read.

HISTORY: *The patient is a 58-year-old married former pharmacist who entered the hospital on 6/22/64 with a history that three weeks ago he had had a fall and hit the left occipital area of his head. One week ago his wife noticed that he could not express himself but could understand what was said. He also showed evidence of confusion. The night before admission he appeared to be having chest pain. His wife noticed a twitching of his left foot. He has lost 20 lbs. in 6 months. In 1960, he reported abdominal pain. In 1962, was treated for cardiac failure. His wife stated for the past 6 months he had occasionally coughed up blood. He takes nitroglycerin tablets for angina twice daily. He has been a heavy smoker for many years.*

This is the first I've heard of it. Any of it. The fall. The nitroglycerin tablets. The heart attack the year I was born. I grip the paper and continue.

PHYSICAL EXAMINATION: *Temperature normal. Weight 130 lbs. Height 5 ft. 10 in. The patient is a confused aphasic male who looks older than his stated age. The eyes were slightly protuberant and slightly widened. Examination of the chest showed diminished breath sounds over the left lung, poor expansion of the chest, poor movement of the diaphragm. Heart sounds were distant. Neurological examination showed slight drooping of the right corner of the mouth. There was questionable grasping reflex of the right hand. The patient was left-handed. Reflexes were more active in the left and left leg. There was marked aphasia.*

All at once, I see my father on the examination table—white gown, silver hair, papery skin, like Howard Brenniman in Hunter, Arkansas, a bag of bones, a specter with my eyes.

HOSPITAL COURSE: *Patient was bronchoscoped on 6/25/64. A tumor mass was found in the right upper lobe. The patient was presented at Chest Conference on 7/2/64, at which time it was agreed that he was not a surgical candidate in view of probable metastatic carcinoma to the brain, as well as heart disease and pulmonary emphysema. After consultation with the Tumor Board, cobalt therapy was started. The patient was seen by a neurosurgeon, who could not differentiate between vascular disease and metastic carcinoma as the patient's mental state continued to deteriorate. Patient received six cobalt treatments before his condition did not permit any further. There was extensive pneumonia for the last two days of his life. He was maintained on IV fluids until 8/8/64, when the patient expired quietly at 3:15 p.m.*

Patient expired quietly. If there is any comfort in this search of mine, maybe this is it. Patient expired quietly.

Folding the letter, I flick off the light.

No. There is no comfort.

My big brother wouldn't cry. Wouldn't look into the open casket. When he knelt before the body at the rosary service, he turned to our middle sister and giggled. "Let's pretend he's alive."

Our sister didn't laugh. Didn't turn away. For years afterward she struggled with what she had been made to see.

❋

Christmas Eve. My father's birthday. I visit my mother's house for the holiday dinner, and to share with my family what I have learned on my trip. I phone my siblings in advance to tell them my plans. They respond with silence, nervous laughter, and cautious curiosity. "Should be interesting."

I creak open the door, unsure how I'll be received, and find my brother sipping Tecate in front of a football game, my sisters joking on the couch, my mother humming an aria in the kitchen, and my uncle sparking a match inside a brown paper luminaria on the porch, his face gold in the evening light.

Tossing aside my jacket, I relax into a corner rocker to soak in the sights and smells of home—steam frosting the windows, piñon incense curling from the floor furnace, and the aroma of garlic, white wine, red chile, and posolé.

When dinner is served, my mother hovers over the table, cheeks flush, flour dusting her hair, giddy from a rum and Coke, too busy to change from her denim housedress.

"More French bread anyone? Tortillas? How's the leg of lamb? Better watch out. That red chile is hot!"

After a few bottles of Merlot, I invite my siblings into the den to share my notes from Arkansas and Iowa. They take their time joining me, stretching, yawning, and patting their bellies before gathering around the manila folders, photographs, and maps I've spread across a floor rug. Our mother collects dishes from the table, "not at all" interested in participating, but humming a little too loudly. My uncle slips out onto the front porch to light more luminarias.

My cheeks burn. I feel like I'm five years old again. I deal snap-shots like poker cards and hurry through a sketchy narrative about the hundred-dollar bill in Hunter, the empty bungalow in Des Moines, and the divorce deposition in Ottumwa. Once finished, I lean back and sigh, ten pounds lighter.

The room is quiet. I tap my pen on my notebook.

"What do you think?

My brother scowls at the images of crumbling cinderblock walls, empty windows, and fallow soybean fields in Hunter.

"What a waste of time," he says, reaching for his motorcycle jacket to leave. "Nothing but a ghost town."

My oldest sister picks at the records as if I'd fished them from the trash, wrinkling her nose, saying nothing.

My middle sister nibbles her thumbnail and watches the older ones to gauge her response. With a forced laugh, she holds up a photocopy of our father's yearbook portrait.

"What a geek. He looks like an elf!"

My youngest sister, a paramedic hoping to study pharmacy, reads the VA form describing his cancer treatment.

"Interesting," she says, holding the paper at arm's length. "Me-tastasized to his brain."

For five or ten minutes we talk as a family about my father for the first time I can remember.

Then it ends.

Our mother calls from the dining room, "Who wants ginger-bread?" and my siblings file away one by one.

Christmas lights blink on and off, yellow and red.

My mother calls again.

Piece by piece, I pack my files away.

❈

My mother's first car was a Cadillac. A silver 1957 Sedan de Ville with white leather interior, dolphin fins, bullet bumpers, and chrome dome hub cabs. My father bought it for her after they married. She felt safe in the heavy, low-slung sedan with power steering, power windows, and v-8 engine. She barely had to tap the accelerator to leave the world behind.

"Just like riding a cloud," she'd say.

I played in the backseat as a toddler. Crawled on plush carpet. Caressed buttery upholstery. Gazed through curved windows at the flash of my father's lighter.

A year or so after his funeral, my mother and I drove home from the grocery store when we rumbled over train tracks. The battery cables jostled loose. The Cadillac stopped dead on the rails. My mother couldn't start the engine, unlock the doors, roll down the windows. Our cries were sealed inside with us. Eventually, a passing motorist pushed us to safety.

Not long after that, my mother let the engine idle while she rushed into the grocery store for a few things. I put my hands on the half-opened window to watch her go, not noticing that one of my sisters had pushed the chrome button to raise the glass. When my mother returned, my fingers were blue.

Worried that the Cadillac was becoming dangerous, she switched off *Captain Kangaroo* one morning, loaded us into the car, and wheeled into an auto dealer across from Doc Holiday's Pawn Shop. The garage smelled of oil. Tools clinked on concrete. My mother stepped out into the cool darkness, jingling her keys. Beside me in the backseat, my middle sister chewed her thumb. My baby sister squeezed her stuffed Thomasina, cat of three lives. I tightened my safety belt.

A salesman appeared. Tall, dressed in gray and black. My mother opened our door, but we stayed put. Forcing a smile, she tugged us out one by one. The salesman laughed.

My uncle's red Volvo slowed to the curb a moment later. Rolling away, I watched through the back window as the salesman waved, then slid into the Cadillac. The brake lights flashed, once, twice, and slipped into shadow.

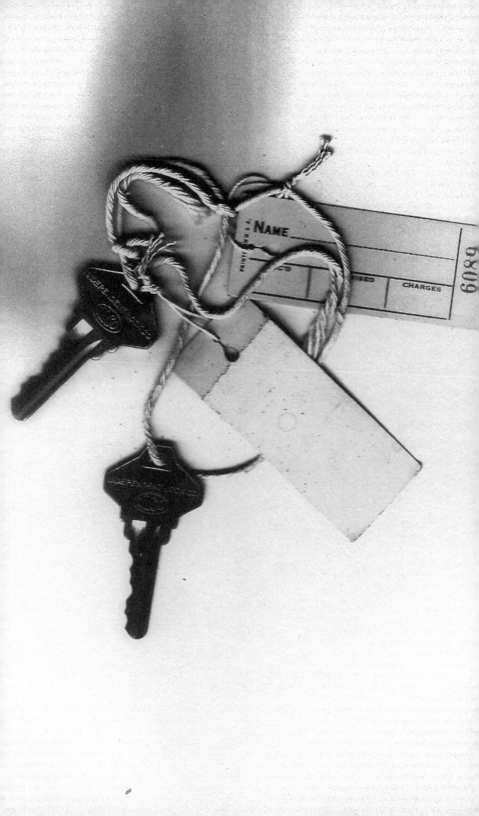

My mother chooses me. She returns home from the feedstore one spring morning with a cardboard box of ducklings and goslings and decides that I, not my big brother or three sisters, will give them food and water and herd them into their pens each night. I complain, but it's not hard. We've adopted a dozen strays since my father died. They wait patiently as I pour corn scratch and lay crumbles into their pans, then waddle to their shelter of wood and straw.

They all like me. All but one. A brooding snow goose that won't let me touch her. Won't run when I yell or stomp. She just lowers her head, spreads her wings, and hisses like an alley cat. When my back is turned, she bites my thigh and twists hard until it swells with blood.

One afternoon when the sun burns like a bare bulb, I shuffle outside to check on the pets. Grass bends rubbery beneath my bare feet. Cicadas grind in the cottonwoods like a headache. Teeth clenched, I unwind the garden hose, turn the spigot, and watch the water flash electric against the feed pan, lulling me into a daydream. I'm Zeus. Burning frustration through his fingers. Raging against his father's ghost, healing himself with fire.

Behind me, I feel a presence, a nudge against my shoulder. I turn and she is there—the snow goose, appraising me with ice blue eyes. Expecting her bite, I flinch, but she leans against me, into me, and nibbles my toes. Unsure what she wants, I pass the nozzle over her back, her wings, her breastbone, her webbed orange feet. I bathe her. She rests her head on my thigh and closes her eyes to sleep. Water dribbles from my hand onto her white flightless feathers.

❋

My mother hung my father's portrait in our living room once. Her younger sister, a budding artist, painted him from a black-and-white snapshot. In the picture, he sat in a smoky blue background wearing a pressed khaki shirt, a thin black tie, a gold Civil Air Patrol pin, and a shiny, black-billed captain's cap with a silver eagle. Unsmiling, arms folded, he looked directly ahead from the poster-sized frame.

His eyes followed me everywhere. When I stood over the floor furnace, or knelt on the rug with my Army men, I felt his steady gaze. When I complained, my mother leaned his portrait against the back wall of our hallway closet.

In its place, she hung a mirror.

❋

My mother dreamed of him for the last time in October 1987, the night before my oldest sister's wedding.

My father knocked on the front door as usual with his thick silver hair and white smoke and waited.

"Go away," my mother told him.

He knocked again.

"No," she said. "I don't believe in you anymore. How can you be who you say you are?"

My mother had recently returned to the church and no longer welcomed his visits.

My father moved to a window, rattled the screen, and told my mother not to let my sister marry. Her fiancé was not right for her. The marriage would end in divorce.

He'd be right, as he always was, but she wouldn't listen.

"Go away," my mother told him. "And don't come back."

My father tried every door and window of our house. He lingered on the porch, waiting for someone to answer.

❋

Early spring. Four months since I shared with my family what I learned on my trip. Four months since I taped shut my cardboard box labeled "Dad." But I haven't stopped thinking about him. Or dreaming about him. Or feeling like I've left something behind, misplaced my keys. One morning after another restless night, I phone my middle sister. Of all my siblings, she talks most easily about our father. Not like the rest of us, in snippets and whispers. When she answers, I blurt out my question: "Do you ever think about him? Dad?"

She pauses, covers the phone with her hand, and mumbles something to her kids before returning.

"Do I ever think about Dad? Yeah. I do."

Steam curls from my coffee cup.

"Really?"

"Sure. But he's always been like a void or a mystery to me. Mom talks about him sometimes, but it's always the same stories told in the same way. Like he's a myth or a fairy tale. Now that my kids are older, they're beginning to ask about him, and I don't know what to say. You know?"

I do know. But I let her talk.

"It's not like Mom withholds, exactly," she continues. "It's more that she doesn't openly share. We always remember Granddad's birthday, or the day Grandma died, but we don't know much about Dad. Like his hair color. I know it was dark, but I don't know if it was black or brown or what. I've tried asking her, but she doesn't understand why I want to know."

Nodding, I sip my coffee, wondering why I've never talked to her like this, and why I, too, have fed the silence.

"I don't feel uncomfortable asking her about him," my sister says, reading my thoughts. "Not like you and the others. I just go ahead and ask. But it's sort of a soft spot with her. Like maybe she feels guilty because she married such an older man. Or because they weren't married in a church. I saw a photo once in the picture box of them in front of a courthouse. I got the sense Grandma didn't approve.

"And you know what else? It's weird, but I only have three memories of him. And I don't even know if they're memories or dreams or what. I remember getting up from bed when I was little and walking into the kitchen. Dad was eating pizza. He sat me on his lap and let me eat all the olives. He thought it was funny, so he called me 'Olive.' Then, a few years ago, I drove Mom to the VA hospital for a doctor's appointment and told her, 'I recognize this place. I remember playing in the grass?' Mom said, 'Yes. I used to bring you here when your father was sick. You kids weren't allowed to play inside, so I left you here to play in the grass. I'd wheel your father to the window and he'd wave to you?' I was all happy because she said it was a real memory."

I stare into the black reflection in my coffee mug, surprised at how much she sounds like me.

"What else did she say?"

"Well, he had four heart attacks. That's why there are no pictures of him with you, me, or us younger ones. He was too sick. They would have had another kid, too, but he had a heart attack in 1960. I always wondered why there was a year gap between the older ones and younger ones. That explains it."

She sips her own coffee.

"They used to fight about his smoking, too. I remember standing in the hallway and singing, 'Daddy don't smoke. Daddy don't smoke?' Mom told me to do that. I remember him sitting on the davenport, watching us, and putting out his cigarette."

She pauses, relieved, it seems, to finally speak aloud.

"I guess I never had problems with him dying because I had closure. You were too young. But I remember sitting on the bunk beds in the boys' room and him telling me something. I ran into the living room and started crying. I sat on the davenport. Mom came over. I climbed in her lap. Then I ran into the front yard. That's when he told me good-bye."

The phone goes quiet. I drain my mug.

"Thanks," I finally say. "I thought I was the only one."

"Hey, no problem," she says through a sigh. "I think about him a lot. You're not alone."

❄

My little sister never dreamed of our father. She was nine months old when he died. Without a single memory, she told me once, what could she dream?

But there was something. Something she believes.

In autumn 1989, she had broken up with her partner. Took it hard. Sat alone in her apartment with a bottle of wine when she heard a knock on her door. She thought it was her ex, so she ignored it. The knock came again, louder.

"Go away!"

The third knock rattled the windows.

My sister stomped to the door and swung it open.

The hallway stood empty.

Puzzled, a little spooked, my sister locked the lock, latched the deadbolt, flicked off the lights, and poured herself another glass. Headlights streaked the walls.

As she considered who might have visited, she remembered what our mother said about her dreams—that our father always knocked when he came, seeking permission to enter.

If it was him, my sister said aloud, if it was our father, then he was welcome. He could come inside.

She began to cry.

At that moment, she felt warmth, as if someone had embraced her.

It was him, my sister told me. She knew it was.

She didn't have to remember.

❄

My father stands beside me on the ditch bank. Silver hair. Laugh lines around his eyes. Instead of a black overcoat he wears a gray-and-white checkered shirt. He is relaxed, grinning, leaning so close I feel his warmth. He is a few inches shorter than me. I never knew that. I smile.

Without a word he glances over my shoulder, reaches behind me, and begins working with his hands. I turn to see what he's doing. Weaving. Pulling long threads through a plain white envelope. Stretching the fibers tight as guitar strings. Shaping them into a cone and gathering the ends.

I reach out to touch the razor-like fibers, but pause and pull back, afraid I might cut myself.

My father nods, continues more slowly, and runs his fingers through the strands as if combing the tangles from a woman's wet hair. He wants

*me to see this. To understand—there is no pain. He steps back and gives
me his work.*

I look into his soft brown eyes. With both hands, I take the knot.

❋

"Guess what? I found your father's ring."

I sit on my mother's porch chewing a mint leaf to mark the changing season. The screen door flaps open and she bounds out holding a purple velvet pouch fastened with a yellow cord.

"Imagine that," she says, sitting beside me. "I was doing some spring cleaning and found it at the bottom of an old drawer. I've always had it. Kept it for you. But I forgot."

My father's ring. My heirloom. I remember seeing it once or twice as a boy while rummaging through my mother's scarf drawer. Heavy, tarnished, it slipped from my finger when I tried it on. Pinged on the hardwood floor and rolled away.

Smiling, she unties the bundle as if removing a suture, and extracts a wide silver band with a square of dark green turquoise split down the middle by a crack.

When I reach for it, she pulls away.

"Wait. Listen."

One afternoon a few years before I was born, a Navajo man visited my father's pharmacy seeking medicine for his ill wife. He didn't have any money, but my father filled the prescription anyway. Touched, the man slipped a ring from his finger and offered it to my father in pawn. My father refused, but the man insisted, so my father placed the jewel in the bottom drawer of his cash register until the man returned.

Year after year he waited, but no one ever claimed the ring, so my father slid it onto his third finger of his right hand, where it stayed until he died.

"See the worn edges," my mother says. "The greasy stone. This was a special ring. Personal. Not the kind they made for tourists. The man who made this rarely took it off."

She drops the heirloom in my palm. It gleams in the noonday sun. With her finger, she smooths the broken stone.

Spring 1957. My father sat alone at the back counter of his drugstore after the death of his second wife. He'd packed her things, cleaned her drawers, polished the hardwood floors, and still he couldn't go home, so he passed another evening with his coffee and cigarettes, watching the dusky sky.

The bell tinkled on his door. A young woman entered. A woman who often stopped by his soda fountain for a sandwich after visiting the library across Route 66. Chestnut hair. Creamy skin. Smoky eyes. A regal bearing, like Grace Kelly.

He watched her, entranced by her beauty, her serenity, and something else, an air of sorrow. He snuffed his Pall Mall and walked over to her stool. Asked if he could join her.

Glancing up, she smiled at his gentle face, dark brooding eyes, and immaculate white smock. My mother extended her hand.

"Renee. My name is Renee."

❧

Dorothy Lawson sits across from me at a café table near my newsroom, fidgeting. A year has passed since I first received her letter. A year since I visited Arkansas and Iowa. A year of wondering how to approach her. I apologize too many times for the delay, thank her again and again for her note, and ask the same questions in different ways, still hungry for details about my father. She does her best to answer, but can only repeat what she'd written. After an hour, I fold an empty sugar packet. She pokes a fork through an uneaten salad.

"Sorry I don't have more," Dorothy says, placing her napkin neatly on her plate. "But I did find this several months ago while going through some old papers."

She reaches into her black handbag, slips out a white envelope, and passes it to me over the table.

I open the flap. Out falls a snapshot of my father.

"I don't know how I got it or where it came from," Dorothy says, smoothing her orange beauty-parlor perm. "But you can have it if you'd like."

I sip ice water. "Thanks."

Patting my hand, she excuses herself to the restroom.

I watch her leave, then angle the black-and-white toward the window. In the snapshot, my father stands before the ivy-covered wall of a house I've never seen wearing a dark gray suit, a black dress shirt, and a thin black tie. His hair is streaked silver. In his left hand, he holds a fedora.

My dreams. They felt so real. He felt so real.

I realize I will never know if my father came to me as he came to my mother, or if my visions were just fragments of fear, guilt, and unexpressed grief. I'd like to believe it was him. And I'd like to believe he finally helped me to see him for who he was—a fifty-eight-year-old pharmacist from Iowa who toward the end of his life was finally given what he most wanted, a family. My father was not a phantom, a myth, or a mystery. He was just a man, haunted by his own ghosts on a journey to find peace. The shadow I have felt so strongly has been my own. By focusing so intently on what I lost, I overlooked all that I truly have. I made my own purgatory of silence. I became the man in the box. And in the end, I believe, this is what he wanted me to find.

I hold the photo closer. At the bottom, I notice a date—April 1957, about the time he met my mother. And this—in the half-dozen images I've seen of him, my father is always turned from the lens, caught in midsentence, awkward, uncomfortable. But here, he looks into the camera, at me.

Here, he is smiling.

ASH

The cottonwoods stand in an alfalfa field beside the Rio Grande, gnarled, twisted, and frozen in death. The color, the bone white of bare wood, catches our eye from the road. We park on the shoulder. White dust hangs in the autumn air.

My uncle goes first, then my big brother, my mother, and my three sisters and me. Ignoring the No Trespassing sign, we squeeze under the rusty barbed-wire fence, scratching our arms and legs before wading into the waist-high grass.

Crows cackle. Crickets dart across our path. All around us, the smell of hot mud and rotting leaves.

Approaching the trees, my family shouts out descriptions as if reading cloud shapes.

"Look," my mother says, pointing to a stump with a knothole at the bottom, a broken branch in the center, and two cracks on either side. "A mouth, nose, and eyes. An old man."

"Here's a dragon," my brother yells, hopping onto a smooth, arching log.

"This one's a chess piece," my uncle adds, touching a narrow, tapered trunk. "A bishop. Or a queen."

My sisters straddle Indian ponies.

I stand before a fallen log split down the middle by a crack as black as a mountain cave. Through the narrow opening, I can see a disc of sunlight, bright as a silver dollar.

The trees have been hollowed out by fire, my uncle explains. Sparked by dry lightning. The bark has been seared away and the insides charred as black as midnight, leaving the naked wood to shine pearly gray as if bathed in moonlight.

"A cottonwood graveyard," he says, laughing.

He and my mother snap art photos while my siblings peek into their dark wooden bowls, dancing and giggling as if they've discovered caldrons of conquistador treasure.

I stare deep into my log, transfixed by the spot of light in the shadow. The crevasse is just big enough for me to fit through, so I wriggle inside. The hollow smells of smoke. The walls are criss-crossed with X's and S's, hieroglyphics or Sanskrit, a language I can't read. Everywhere ash and soot.

Scooting through the tight tube, I scrape my elbows and knees. Sweat dribbles down my stomach. My eyes sting. I can't breathe. Can't see. Everything spins. Blackens.

Suddenly, I feel my toes prickle, stretch, and spiral through loam and clay, seeking the pulse of the river. My fingers stiffen, thin, extend into branches, into stems, reaching toward the sun. I sense the itch of a carpenter ant, the tickle of sap, the warmth of buried stones.

"Where is he?" My mother's voice is muffled, distant. "Where did he go?"

I open my eyes and glance up toward an oval of turquoise sky clear as a phoenix eye. Pushing against the wood with my feet and hands, I inch forward until someone grabs my wrist and pulls me out onto the warm alfalfa.

"Look. He's all dirty!" My brother slugs my shoulder.

My mother frowns at the scratches on my arms and face.

"Why did you go in there?"

I just smile at her, caressing the ash and blood.

RINGS

I drive across the desert to see her, six hundred round trip from Santa Fe to Las Cruces, from the city of holy faith to the city of three crosses. On warm spring nights I pull back the bedsheets in her college apartment to watch the light from the streetlamp pool in her belly.

"You're so shy," she whispers. "When we make love, you hardly make a sound."

"What am I supposed to say?"

Grinning, she presses a finger to my lips and pulls me so close I can see myself in her eyes.

"Maybe it will be me," she says. "Maybe I'll be the one to break your shell."

❋

I watch from the shadows of the capitol rotunda as she crosses the white marble floor. Rosebud lips. Egyptian eyes. A grace I will never possess. She walks in circles looking for my office and gasps when I finally call her name. With both hand she takes hold of my own, then pulls me into the light.

❋

My uncle, an artist, will make our wedding rings, heavy gold bands with delicate pierce-work symbols resembling Aramaic, Sanskrit, ancient Greek, Arabic, or hieroglyphics.

"Lovely," my fiancée says, examining the designs under my uncle's worktable light. "But couldn't we have something simpler? More traditional? Matching?"

I fold my arms. "Who cares if they match? I want something different. Something distinctive."

She clicks her tongue, selects a pattern at random, and excuses herself. I watch her leave before choosing a design resembling a labyrinth or maze, struck by one particular symbol—a crescent with four radiating lines, a rising sun or a setting sun, a winking eye or a closed eye, my fiancée when she kisses me, or has something difficult to say.

❀

We marry on Memorial Day weekend in a courtyard of cottonwoods and sunflowers beside the Rio Grande. Red rose petals sprinkle the tables. When the champagne pops, I raise a goblet for a toast. My bride steps forward, radiant in handmade lace, and extends her glass through the space between us. Above the cheers I hear a ping, feel a splash, and see the glint of my goblet stand rolling across the floor. I kneel before anyone notices to pocket the broken disc.

❀

I spin the wedding band on my finger. Slide it off. Slip it on again. My wife watches me over a plate of linguine with salmon cream sauce on the first day of our honeymoon. Twice as wide as a normal band, and twice as heavy, my ring catches on my pants pocket when I dig for keys, clicks against my beer glass when I reach for a sip, and bruises my right palm when I clap. It's tarnished, too, more brassy than golden. I rub it with my shirttail again and again, and still it's cloudy. My wife's band, meanwhile, gleams on her finger like the ray of sunlight slanting through her glass of Chardonnay.

"Well, that's what you wanted," she says, raising an eyebrow while I fidget. "Something different. Distinctive."

"You're right," I say, hiding my hand beneath the table. "It just doesn't feel right. I can't get used to it."

My wife sets down her fork to examine her own ring. She's not sure she likes hers either, she says, fanning her long thin fingers. She might have picked the wrong design.

We stare at our food.

To break the silence, I mention the next day's itinerary. While my wife details a museum visit, I slip my hand beneath the table, remove the gold band, and rub it with my napkin.

✷

Late autumn. A concrete sky. My wife sits beside me on our new apartment couch hugging her knees. In place of her wedding band, she wears the star sapphire her mother had given her before she died. My wife wears it when the anniversary of the funeral approaches. When I reach out to touch the pale blue stone, the ring spins loosely on her finger.

"Beautiful," I say. "Too bad it doesn't fit. Maybe I can fix it for you. With a little strip of tape."

She slips her hand beneath a pillow.

"No. It fits fine."

✷

My father left me a ring. A square of green turquoise cracked down the middle. It slides off when I wear it. I've tried tape around the edges. Even a Band-Aid. Nothing works. The space is too big for me to fill.

✷

My wife and I work in the same office. The man in the cubicle between us pops his chewing gum when he smiles and wears no wedding ring, although he's married with a two-year-old daughter. Each morning he shares coffee with my wife. In the afternoons, they have long lunches.

He's simple. Traditional. Comfortable in his own skin, she tells me. Like her. Like her mother. Not like me.

I play pool with him sometimes after work. I sip warm Guinness stout and choke on cigarette smoke while he peels his Coors Lite label and winks at the waitresses.

He outshoots me rack after rack.

✷

"Must be a chemical on my skin," I tell my mother and uncle. "I've been married nine months and my ring is still tarnished. The symbols are practically black."

My mother squints at my band under the worktable light. She can polish it, she says, but it's perfectly natural. In fact, in her eyes, the tarnish gives my ring character.

"Keep wearing it," she says. "It will brighten."

❋

I visit my middle sister while my wife works late. I sit cross-legged on my sister's carpet while my niece and nephew watch Disney cartoons. Of all my four siblings, my middle sister is the only one still married. The others are divorced, single, or involved with difficult partners.

"It's strange about the relationships in our family," I say after a while. "How they never seem to last. I don't even remember Mom's wedding ring. After Dad died, I don't remember seeing it. For all I know, she even never had one."

My sister examines her own gold band, which cuts into her finger. "Not true," she says. "I saw it once on Mom's dresser when I was little. It was gold. Simple. But distinctive. She had a pearl engagement ring, too. Dad took a photo of Mom once dressed like a señorita. She wore the rings in it. Remember?"

As soon as she spoke, I did remember. In the portrait, our father hand-tinted the rings electric yellow. Our mother held her left hand to her chin, gathering a black veil.

❋

"Don't wait up," my wife tells me over the phone. "I'll be working late."

I wait up anyway, clicking buttons on the TV remote.

After the ten o'clock news, I dial her number. No answer. I call again, then try her pager. Still no response.

At the office, I find her desk empty, her coffee cold.

Returning to our apartment, I find her leaning toward the bathroom mirror applying face lotion. She'd gone for a drive after work to clear her head, she said. She didn't get my messages. She'd forgotten her pager.

When she closes the door, I lift her purse from the kitchen table. Inside I find the pager beside the office badge of the man who pops his gum, the ringer switched off.

❋

Memorial Day weekend. Our wedding anniversary. While my wife packs her things to move out, I drive fast along the river's edge. Steeple bells ring from behind a wall of cottonwoods. I hit the gas, but can't escape the echo.

❋

My mother arrives at my new apartment with a child's wagon of potted ferns, garden tools, and shopping bags from Target. Housewarming gifts, she says with a hug.

I follow her around as she arranges tables and chairs, slips on new bedsheets, hangs white cotton curtains, and plants sod, mint, and periwinkle in my fenced courtyard.

Before leaving, she places a cactus on the windowsill.

"Water it," she tells me. "But not too much."

❋

As a boy I stood beside the Rio Grande skipping stones to the opposite bank. Three splashes and I always fell short. For hours I watched ripples radiate across the glassy brown surface, rooted to the sand, willing them to reach the shore.

❋

"There are no guarantees," the priest tells me.

"No guarantees," my wife echoes.

"Faith," the priest continues. "You must have faith. And above all, trust. There must be trust."

"Trust," my wife says, nodding. "Trust."

We stand at the altar of the church where we were married, preparing to renew our vows.

The priest faces me. "Do you understand?"

Dust hangs in the scented air.

I nod to my wife and look down at her ring.

She laces her trembling fingers.

❊

We stumble in a daze into Denver, a city we've circled on a map. At night we lie back to back and stare at our walls.

And yet, at times, through the darkness we touch.

❊

My mother tells me a story: as a girl she wandered into the llano beyond the call of her grandmother and mother. Even whistles bent on the howling wind. Among the red sand and cholla cactus, she listened for the ring of a cast-iron church bell radiating toward her in ever-widening circles.

She was patient, she said. Always, it would come.

❊

When our daughter is born I am the first to hold her. In the hospital's lavender light, her pupils swallow shape and shadow. She looks at me, into me, I slide forever into the pools of her eyes.

❊

A surprise Christmas gift for my wife: a sapphire surrounded by diamonds and mounted on a simple, traditional silver band, sized to fit her finger.

"Lovely," she says. "Like my mom's. Almost."

She extends her hand.

The stone flashes in the morning light.

❊

Our daughter will be baptized by the priest who married us and renewed our vows. Before the service, I reach into a black velvet box for my wedding band, sliding it on for the first time in two years. It fits. The only ring that does.

✻

Outside our Denver home, wind strips leaves from the front yard maples. Yellow shards fill the sky. Beneath our living room window, a rose blooms in the late autumn light. Bright pink, edged in frost, it taps the glass while I sit with my wife stroking her hair to help her sleep. The anniversary of her mother's death has come and gone.

"Bring it inside," she says of the rose. "With us."

✻

On All Souls' Day our son is born. Choose his name carefully, our priest says. Words bind, reverberate.

My wife favors something simple, biblical, while I prefer the distinctive, the symbolic.

We call him Cruz. Cross. Suffering. Hope.

ONE PRAYER

I arrive at Tomé Hill in the blue-black of dawn. Already the trail is crowded. A catering truck dispenses breakfast burritos beneath a Pete's Carpeting banner, two Valencia County deputies yawn from their patrol car bumper, and an Action Seven News van raises its dish for a live satellite feed. All around me, dozens of men, women, and children shuffle through the powdery dirt with white Styrofoam cups of cocoa or coffee. And everyone, it seems, holds a rosary, hand-hewn crucifix, vial of holy water, or bouquet of roses. Everyone but me. Once again, I've come empty-handed.

✳

Ten years earlier. Holy Week, 1994. While researching a newspaper column about the annual pilgrimage to Tomé Hill, an event I'd heard about all my life but never attended, historians directed me to Edwin Berry, who erected three larger crosses on the summit four decades earlier. Berry would be happy to help, he told me over the phone, but only if I would accompany him on a hike to the peak. I agreed.

Pebbles skittered from our path as we climbed above the patchwork of corn and alfalfa fields twenty-five miles southeast of Albuquerque. Berry kept a good pace. At seventy-five, with feathery white hair, a generous belly, and wearing cowboy boots, a button-up shirt and a brown fedora with a red feather, he hardly paused for breath as he explained the history of the procession in a slow raspy twang.

Visitors have been drawn to Tomé Hill for centuries, he said, his face as wrinkled as a leather work glove, in part because it's a geographic anomaly, a mound of basalt and volcanic rock rising three hundred feet from the valley floor, the only rise in the fifteen miles of flatland between the Rio Grande and the Manzano foothills. The Anasazi came first, then the conquistadores, and eventually Los Hermanos de Penitentes, a secretive Catholic lay order that planted a single cross at the peak on Easter and sang hymns at sunrise.

The higher we rose above the valley, the deeper I entered Berry's world. He seemed to know the name and origin of every plant, rock, and animal on the hill. The land seemed to speak to him as it spoke to my mother—in a language I couldn't quite understand. As we cleared the first rise, he plucked a spiral shell from the trail and rolled it in his palm—the husk of a desert worm residing everywhere on the hill. In the sand. Beneath the chamisal. Even on the faces of the ancient petroglyphs, etched white into the purple rock.

"It is the wheel of life," Berry said, returning the pea-sized shell where he found it, continuing up the slope. "On Tomé Hill, on El Cerro, everything has meaning."

I scribbled in my notebook as if I understood, then followed.

❋

The crowd grows at the trailhead. I park on the roadside, step out, and wade through the knee-high grass, struck instantly by the smell of irrigated soil, a smell more healing to me than eucalyptus balm.

I'd left Denver a day earlier in a mumble of apologies to my wife and two children, who stood on our porch in the morning air, asking me to stay. I smoothed their hair, kissed their cheeks, and promised them a surprise. My wife told me to be careful and closed the door. I drove in a daze to central New Mexico, 480 miles straight down Interstate 25, the asphalt umbilical cord linking one home to another, called by a feeling I can neither define nor dismiss.

Gazing east of the trailhead, I see my destination a half-mile away—three black crosses pressed like swords into the summit. Gathering my jacket against the wind, I approach.

Berry talked nonstop while we climbed, his bushy white eyebrows perpetually raised as if surprised by his own memory. I scrambled to keep up, stumbling over the rocks in our path.

As we neared the second rise, he paused, set down a plastic water jug he'd carried beneath his left arm, and selected a pebble from the dirt. He turned the gray-black stone in his fingers as if examining a lucky penny, tucked it in his shirt pocket, and resumed his story.

His father might have been a Penitente, he said, although his family was never sure. His father memorized Bible verses each night, kissed the rings of elders he called "hermano," and helped dig graves for poor families—the telltale duty of the devout order. Mostly, Berry recalled, his father sang Spanish hymns as they herded sheep to the Manzanos. Alabados, his father called them, songs of the heart.

At night, when his father retreated to the Rio Grande bosque to pray, Berry followed without permission. Through the darkness, he heard his father's clear voice rising from the secluded morada chapel. That's how he found his father in the pitch-black forest, Berry told me. He followed the songs.

❀

Pilgrims hurry up the trail to catch the sunrise. The sky glows green and yellow. I pick up my pace as well, passing the burrito truck and news van before pausing near the base of the hill at a small barrier of concrete, stone, and wood—a gateway I recognize from my first visit years earlier.

Silently, I read the words etched into the cement: "Fear the Lord," "Sin No More," and "Repent"—the admonitions of Berry, who wrote them, he told me, to remind those who joined the pilgrimage to understand the meaning of their actions.

Shifting my weight, I feel uncomfortable. Like a tourist. A fraud. I glance back at the deputies, half-expecting them to check my credentials. When one nods at me, I look away.

❈

I left the church at age eight, following my mother, a lifelong Catholic, who had drifted away for reasons I never knew. As with most things I didn't understand about her, I assumed it had to do with my father's death.

If I asked her today, thirty-five years later, she would say that her departure had nothing to do with my father, that she'd never questioned her faith, that she didn't agree with the liberalization of Catholic doctrine during the Vatican II Council, and that she had simply sought a traditional mass with a traditional priest and traditional sermon. She would say that I'm distorting history. And maybe I am. But I remember her leading me through the parking lot of Our Lady of Guadalupe church one autumn evening after Chicano boys had bullied me over my shoulder-length hair. She said I didn't have to go back if I didn't want to. I said I didn't want to.

From my time in catechism, I recall only this: coloring faded blue dittos of Jesus and the apostles, sliding on my knees across the glossy floor of the church gym, and wearing an orange paisley neck scarf instead of a black tie for my First Holy Communion. I know only one prayer: Our Father.

❈

A wrinkled farmer wearing a bolo tie and a straw cowboy hat extends his hand for me to enter through the concrete gateway of El Cerro, but I step aside to let him pass. Several others file through as well, marching toward the summit in a line of black dots reminding me of ants approaching a picnic.

The sun breaks over the Manzanos, magenta and gold.

I step from the path to make my own way. On this pilgrimage, I decide, I'll walk alone.

❈

As a young man Berry was gifted with a singing voice, like his father. But unlike his father, he was more interested in popular ballads than Penitente songs, although his father often implored him to "keep the prayers alive" and "never let the alabados die."

After World War II, Berry returned to Tomé suffering from malaria and chronic nightmares. He sought solace in whiskey. On the first Holy Week of his return, Berry and his father climbed El Cerro. At the summit they found no Penitente cross, no offering, no sign of the dwindling Penitente Brotherhood. Filled with a sorrow and longing he could not define, Berry vowed to stop drinking, restore the cross, and revive the Good Friday procession.

He began work in March 1946 hauling lumber, cement mix, and water buckets to the summit, where he built an altar of concrete and stone and three crosses of railroad ties and sheet metal. The largest stood sixteen feet tall. He painted it silver. The others stood fifteen feet. He painted them red. Each was positioned to match the crosses at Mount Calvary in Jerusalem, where Jesus was crucified.

A year later, Berry again climbed El Cerro with his father. On Easter morning, they sang.

❊

Shale crunches beneath my boots, sliding away with the tinkle of broken glass. In the still air of El Cerro, sound is magnified. Six stories above the valley, I can hear a goat bleating from its pen, a screen door slamming on a trailer, and a tractor grinding to life in the fields, all funneled here, all absorbed by the body of the hill. And there's this, too—voices, songs, or prayers, I can't tell which, can't discern the words, so I close my eyes, stop in my tracks, and listen.

❊

In retrospect, I could have returned to mass on my own, asked my mother to teach me prayers, or picked up a Bible. But in truth, I didn't miss it. Not really. There were things I enjoyed about church, like the incense and the stained-glass windows, but I was quite content to sleep late on Sundays and scoot in front of the TV for *Underdog* and *Space Ghost*. I was more than happy to be the son of an artist, activist, and woman who thought and acted differently from any other mom at school. When I grew up, I wanted to be just like her.

Still, I'd sometimes steal away with the glow-in-the-dark rosary my grandmother gave my big sister. I'd hold it over a living room lamp until the plastic beads became too hot to hold. Then I'd sneak it under my bedcovers to watch the globes burn a whitish-green. I'd fall asleep with the crucifix in my hands, watching it fade.

❋

One spring day in 1953, Berry stood atop a ladder plastering a house. He'd stopped drinking as promised, landed a construction job, launched a part-time singing career, married an Italian woman he'd met during the war, and had four sons. He'd even begun cataloging old Penitente songs. His life, he thought, had been truly blessed. But as he filled his trowel on that clear morning, the sun seemed to dim. He became dizzy and fell. When he woke, he'd gone "black-velvet blind."

Doctors diagnosed him with a malaria relapse and delayed war trauma, but no amount of medicine, rest, or counseling helped. He entered a psychiatric hospital. Months passed.

One night, from the fog of nightmares and sweat, he heard singing. At first, Berry thought it was a nurse, but the more he listened, the clearer the sound became. Little by little, he recognized melodies, words, hymns, alabados. He began to hum. When he opened his eyes, he could see.

❋

Halfway to the summit, I stumble upon a middle-aged woman and a teenage girl. The woman is short, thin, and dressed in white jeans, jacket, and athletic shoes. Her eyes are swollen from crying. In her left hand she holds a portrait of a grade-school boy, dark hair neatly parted.

"How long have we been walking?" The woman wheezes.

"It was dark when we left," the girl says. "Three hours?"

The woman coughs a rough, wet cigarette cough. For a moment, I wonder if she will turn back.

"We're almost there," the girl says, placing a hand on the mother's back. "Look. The sun's coming up."

The woman faces the orange sky. Taking the girl's hand, she squares her shoulders and continues.

As they clear the first rise, I take their path.

❋

Although my family no longer attended mass, my mother showed me her spirituality in other ways, especially during weekend excursions into the countryside. As often as not, we wound up at an abandoned church or forgotten cemetery, which held more history, she'd say, than any of my schoolbooks.

She was right. But I also wondered if she chose those destinations for other reasons. When I stood beside her in a windswept camposanto reading Spanish names carved in stone, she'd pull a dried root from the sand and touch my shoulder.

"Look at the color," she'd say, studying its contours under the noonday sun. "Blue-black and ash gray. Like a tree branch at night. And see the twisted shape? Like a rattlesnake. Or a river. Now smell the dirt. Like gunpowder. Or the air after a lightning storm. Isn't it gorgeous?"

I'd study the root as she spoke, nodding as if I saw what she did, marveling at how she could find so much life in a dead thing. And when she'd enter a chapel, I'd follow close behind, breathing in the dusty sweetness of old wood and votive candles, lingering in the threshold as she creaked across the wooden floor, waiting for my eyes to adjust.

❋

After clearing the first rise, I detour north on El Cerro to explore a meadow. Tufts of chamisal ripple in the breeze. Slowing my pace, I gather artifacts like my mother. I pull strands of buffalo grass, roll a gray stone in my palm, and select two dried twigs, which I cross into a "t," a small crucifix that will become my offering, I decide, for the altar. But I need something more, something to complete the gift, a flower. Head down, I comb the ground.

❄

An hour, Berry and I reached the summit.

"Look around you," he said, sweeping a hand over the rolling plains. "No walls. No roof. No utility bills. No parish council. Just the sun, sky, and land. And El Cerro is always open. It is the perfect church."

Smiling at my puzzled expression, Berry shuffled away to perform his caretaker's duties—checking the votive candles flickering in the sheet-metal shrine, returning a pink rosary to its nail on the silver cross, and brushing faded red carnation petals from the stone nicho. Everything in order, he fished into his shirt pocket for the pebbles he had collected earlier, and laid them on the altar.

"For my friends," he said.

Next, Berry reached for the plastic water jug he had been carrying. Instead of taking a drink as I had expected, he bent over a cluster of violet irises beneath the sheet-metal shrine and poured a long silvery stream.

"I planted them a few years ago," he explained. "I picked purple— the color of royalty. Each year they bloom on Holy Week. I didn't plan it that way, but it happens."

Tasks complete, Berry settled beside me in the shade of the silver cross and fanned himself with his fedora. A cloud of butterflies drifted toward us from the meadow below.

"Must be the irises," I said. "The pollen."

"No." Berry squinted at a monarch settling on a stone near our feet. "When you see one like this, it's a sign. There's a soul who wants you to pray for it."

He slid from the boulder and knelt on all fours.

"Pardon, señor," he whispered, placing his forehead in the dust. "I come to implore your forgiveness."

The butterfly remained absolutely still.

Berry closed his eyes, and began to sing.

❄

A stone skitters to my left. I look up from the meadow and into the face of an angel—a girl of four or five wearing a white nylon gown, a pair of white nylon wings, and a wire halo decorated with white feathery fuzz. Her hair is long and dark and her brown eyes big and serious.

"Hello," I say. "I like your costume."

She jumps, startled, as if she didn't see me.

"Your costume is very pretty," I try again.

Appraising me, she walks barefoot across the rocky ground before kneeling at a bush I mistook for a weed. She turns from me, picks a lavender blossom, holds it up, and smiles.

❋

My mother returned to the church in the fall of 1989, as I remember it, a year after I'd left home for Southern California. Her father lay in a hospital bed suffering through the final stages of Parkinson's while she recovered a few floors down from him with a blood clot in her thigh. She could have a stroke, doctors said. She might die.

One night, a priest visited to administer last rites.

But she'd left the church years ago, she told him.

Had she been baptized a Catholic? he asked.

Yes, she replied.

Did she make her First Holy Communion? Confirmation?

Yes. She'd been a Catholic most of her life.

Then she was still a Catholic, the priest said. And always would be.

They talked for hours.

By sunrise, she'd made her peace.

❋

The summit looms before me, fifty yards ahead. Off the main path, directly below the three crosses, I notice a crowd gathered in a circle. A teenage girl covers her mouth with her hand. A rancher removes his cowboy hat and places it over his chest. I hurry forward to see what happened.

A man has stumbled. He leans forward in the dirt on his hands and knees, gray hair matted, sweatshirt dusty, bare feet smeared with blood. His chest heaves, and his forehead shines with sweat, but no one offers to help. When I reach out, he pushes up, straightens his back, and reaches beside him for an eight-foot wooden cross made of heavy lumber. Grunting, he lifts the weight onto his left shoulder, gritting his teeth.

The crowd parts for him, and the man crawls forward, nodding to me as he passes.

❈

In November 1996, Berry suffered a stroke. He couldn't move. Couldn't speak. That spring, as Good Friday approached, I met with his oldest son, Dante, who had agreed to replace his father in the annual procession. But he wasn't ready, Dante told me. At thirty-six, a father himself, he didn't think he ever would be. As we sat in my car at the base of El Cerro, Dante opened a file folder in his lap.

"When I was a kid, I doubted him," he said, thumbing through a stack of yellowed news clippings. "I never had any interest in what he was doing. I thought he made up all that Penitente stuff. I mean, who could memorize two hundred old songs? I always thought someone else would carry on the tradition. I never thought it would be me."

Dante pointed to a front-page photograph from 1965 of him on the summit in his father's lap, the elder pointing to a rock or a shrub, and explaining something to his scowling son.

"That's the last time I walked this hill willingly with him," Dante said. "I was four years old."

After a long silence, we hiked the path I had taken with his father three years earlier. I gave Dante a wide berth. He sighed. Shook his head. Rattled pebbles in his palm. Combed the dry range grass as if searching for lost keys.

"To a lot of people this is just a hill with three crosses on it," Dante said to himself as much as me. "But to my father, it was sacred. He'd look at a bush and say, 'This is food for some animal.' He'd see a rabbit dropping and say, 'This, too, has significance.' To him, everything was in harmony. But I never allowed myself to see it."

At the altar, he knelt in the sand to pray for his father, for forgiveness, for guidance, for everything I, too, had wanted to say about my own father but could not express.

"I am not Edwin Berry," Dante mumbled, shaking his head. "I will help out all I can, but I will never replace him. All I want to do is learn one song. Just one song."

He walked to the edge of the summit and gazed down at his village. Eyes closed, he waited for the wind to still, then in a clear voice, began to sing.

❋

Pilgrims watch me. I linger too long at the altar. I try to concentrate but there's too much commotion—a man plucking an acoustic guitar, two teenage girls yakking on cell phones, a sullen boy lugging a boom box, a tourist clicking a digital camera, and a man with a Lakers jersey restraining a pit bull on a heavy chain. Behind me, a woman clucks her tongue. A man grumbles. I feel their eyes prodding me to get on with it.

Before taking my place in line, I had scribbled the names of my wife, children, mother, and father on a scrap of notebook paper and tucked it into my crucifix of twigs and flowers.

Breathing deep, I place my offering on the metal shrine and recite my one prayer. Wind rattles the rosaries on the silver cross. The woman shuffles her feet. The man groans.

❋

When I returned to my mother's home after five years in Southern California, I found framed prints of Christ in place of Navajo rugs. On the TV, Mother Angelica instead of CNN.

One evening, my mother invited her new priest to join us for supper. He sat at the head of the table, a stern but jovial New Yorker with steel-blue eyes and silver-rimmed glasses. I sat at his right, as my mother requested.

During the meal he spoke about politics and society, praising men who shot abortion doctors and ridiculing liberals, artists, and news reporters. My mother glowed.

Over pie and coffee, the priest cleared his throat.

"Your son hasn't spoken all night," he said. "It's the quiet ones we have to watch out for, isn't it?"

My mother set down her fork and lowered her eyes.

"Yes," she said. "It is."

❋

I step from the altar and start down the slope with quick strides, when I hear a drumbeat from the meadow below—a low boom rising on the wind and settling in deep my belly. In the distance, I see three men and three boys kneeling before a large handheld crucifix with a line of pilgrims behind them. Leading the procession, Dante. I stop in my tracks, and wait.

When the group reaches the summit, the drum beats once and falls silent. I slip into the crowd behind the sheet-metal shrine. Sage smoke curls into the clear blue sky. Dante reads a Bible passage in Spanish. His companion sings an alabado. Beside me, a cotton-haired woman raises her palms to the sun, and a broad-shouldered workman begins to cry. I place my hand on the silver cross. For a moment, I feel it, too.

❋

On the mantel of my Denver bungalow I have arranged my mother's gifts—a wrought-iron crucifix, a strand of Tibetan prayer beads, an ashen bowl for burning piñon incense, a chamisal root, a crystal ball. One evening after my wife and I first moved in, a friend stopped by for a visit.

"Wow," he said. "I didn't know you were so religious."

Taken aback, I blinked. "Why do you say *that?*"

"Your things," he said, laughing. "Look at your things."

I didn't know what to say, except, "They remind me of home."

❋

The ceremony ends. After the crowd clears I approach Dante, who shakes my hand and looks me in the eye. He's not sure if I know this, he says, but each Good Friday since his father's death, he has carried a stone to the summit of El Cerro for my intentions. He fumbles in his shirt pocket and opens his hand to reveal to a dusty brown pebble.

"For you," he says, studying my response.

I look down and swallow hard.

Dante pats my shoulder as if to say no words are necessary, I belong. Then he turns, stands beneath the silver cross, and places my stone upon the altar.

UNDERCURRENT

1

The acequia unwinds before me like a bull snake in the grass. I quicken my pace to catch her but my wife just lengthens her strides, stretching the distance between us. Married only nine months and already I'm losing sight of a woman who once filled my eyes so completely. I've disturbed her solitude again, interrupted her evening jog, and she runs hard after her mother's ghost, as hard as I chase my father's, pursuing a vision I cannot yet see. I catch her at a turn in the ditch bank beneath a canopy of cottonwoods, stroking a pottery shard kicked loose from its shallow grave. I reach out to touch it, to take it, but her fingers curl like a spider, into a fist, and she bolts into the long blue shadows.

Watching her, I hesitate, then follow along the water's edge.

2

The water arrives with the light, with the blue and red of dawn, flowing south from the Rio Grande through the acequia arteries, into hand-dug furrows of alfalfa, corn, beans, and squash, down to the roots of the valley.

My uncle senses it coming, rising with the first window curtain glow to clamp a crescent wrench onto a rusty headgate bolt behind our house. I hear him then, his toenails scratching his denim jeans, his pocket change spilling like stars, and slip on my cutoffs to join him outside, where goose bumps pop like dandelions across my bare arms and legs.

Our geese notice first, then our ducks, guinea hen, and peacock. They charge the acequia with squeaks and squeals and fine silver spray. Toes deep in the wet earth, I wade into the current beside them, awake, alive, green.

3

The acequia gurgles beneath us, green with spring rain. I sit with my girlfriend, my first girlfriend, on a footbridge near our high school. Close your eyes, she tells me, and we kiss. I taste strawberries. Smell the musk of fertile mud.

Parting from her embrace, I grip the plank with my right hand and reach down with my left, palm flat, inches above the current. Then I feel it—trembling air, the water breathing.

4

It has a life of its own, my uncle says. An hour after he opens the headgate, the irrigation water meanders through our backyard, saturates the soil, spills into the front yard driveway, pours into the gutters, and flows halfway around the block. Neighbors complain. The ditch boss threatens. Classmates tease me at school. Shovel in hand, brooding like a shepherd, my uncle fortifies berms, digs trenches, closes the headgate an hour early, and still our property floods.

In time, the streetlamp leans at the curb, peach trees split with rotten fruit, and red ants drown in their holes.

5

Blood fills my head as I pull back on the chains to block out the sun with my Keds. My sister rises in the swing beside me, yowling along to The Beatles. Our mother prunes a rosebush nearby. Her shoulders glisten with baby oil.

"Hush," she says suddenly, facing the ditch behind us.

I plant my feet and follow her eyes. A man slumps beneath an elm watching us. His hair is greasy, his wet lips twist into a smile. At his side, a bottle in a brown paper bag.

My mother scoops up my sister, yanks me inside the kitchen, and locks the door behind us. "He's here again," she whispers into the phone. "Same one as last week."

I scramble to the back bedroom and peek through a hole in the window screen. The man rises, turns toward the kitchen, wipes his mouth, and sings, "I wanna hold your hand."

6

He approaches with open hands but I don't see him at first because I'm burying nail-studded boards behind the fence to discourage firewood thieves. I glance up and he's there-an apparition in rags, a shadow against the blue-red sky.

I've seen him before shuffling along Guadalupe Trail from the bar at Valley Bowl. He's saying something, asking me something, chewing sticky words in his knothole mouth.

I lean into the gate, but he keeps coming, boots stirring little clouds of dust. A nail gleams in the dusky light, a sliver spike against his leather sole. He steps into it, onto it, full weight on right foot, and shivers in silent pain.

Our eyes meet then, and a current forms between us, my fear, his regret, and he retreats up the ditch bank, hands in his pockets, blood in his tracks.

7

My grandfather cut our first ditch, dragged his shovel blade in a straight line from our back fence to the neighborhood acequia, linking our land to the Rio Grande. My father flicked away his cigarette and joined in. Together they dug through sand and clay, unlikely partners, the construction worker from Corrales and the pharmacist from Des Moines, both fifty-two, brought together by my young mother, who was pregnant with her first child, my brother.

Halfway through the job, my grandfather's shovel clipped something hard, not a root or a stone, but a ring, shining in the mud like an eye. He plucked it free and wiped it clean—a white-gold band stamped with the profile of Montezuma or Cortés, its features blurred by water and time.

My grandfather didn't wear jewelry, since he worked with his hands, so he gave the band to my father, who slipped it onto his right ring finger as a keepsake for future children.

I saw my heirloom once while rummaging through my mother's makeup drawer. I don't remember its face, either.

8

Benicio couldn't see her face, but he could hear her whimpering from the bushes as he stumbled down the ditch bank to piss. He was drunk, again, and had been kicked out of the dance hall for bothering women, again. After his third bottle of wine, he just wanted sleep. Despite his mother's warnings and the stories he'd heard all his life, he took a shortcut on the acequia from Alameda to Corrales through the tangled Rio Grande bosque. As midnight approached, he was almost home.

"Buenas noches," said Benicio, my mother's uncle. "What are you doing in there hiding in the bushes like that?"

The woman, it sounded like a woman, began to sob.

"Come out." Benicio laughed. "I won't bite."

Stumbling, he parted the branches to reveal a birdlike woman with her head and shoulders covered in tattered black lace. As he reached out, she parted her veil.

A skull grinned at him, bright as the moon.

"Dios mio!"

Benicio ran. Like a wild horse he ran. The woman flew after him with owl's wings. Three times she swooped down on him, and three times he beat her back with bloody fists.

Finally, in the green light of dawn, he reached his mother's ranch and crashed onto the front porch, clawing at the door. Before he slipped inside, Benicio wheeled around to face his demon, but there was only the rustle of leaves, the scent of smoke, and the echo of laughter.

9

The witch cackles from the poster at school, "Ditches are deadly. Stay away!" We swim in them anyway, although I can't swim. My mother doesn't like the city pools with their chlorine water as blue as the eyes of rich kids, so she drives us to a secluded acequia near Alameda. Hidden behind a wall of cottonwoods, she spreads a towel on the hood of her Comet, slices a watermelon, and watches us from the shade.

My big brother leaps in first, shirtless and tanned, slipping through the ruddy water as quick as a trout.

"Look at me!" He grips a driftwood log as if it were a paddleboard. "I'm Tarzan!"

My sisters go next, clucking like geese, their pale limbs slipping beneath the glassy surface.

I enter last, gripping the ditch bank reeds for balance. I'll be okay, I tell myself, as long as I can touch the bottom and bounce to the other side, as weightless as Neil Armstrong on the moon.

As I approach the middle, water laps at my chin. The undercurrent pulls strong. My toes claw at the mud. I begin to drift. I pump my legs, flail my arms, but lose my footing and slip under anyway, swallowing deep.

I bob to the surface a moment later, gagging, as a shadow drifts toward me. I think it's the log, so I reach out, but my mother screams, and I stop short. A rat floats by, inches from my face, belly to the sun, grinning with orange teeth.

10

Each autumn, when jack-o'-lanterns blaze, an emptiness fills the acequias. I avoid the ditches then, and the shadow men hunkered inside sucking dreams through brown paper bags. I wait until Good Friday, when the hard hats arrive with axes, shovels, and propane torches, rushing outside to watch them behind the silver diamonds of our chain-link fence. Bottles burst. Thorns sizzle. Ash rises on the heat into the cloudless sky, drifting down like feathers.

11

Cottonwoods bloom around us, the air thick with feathery seeds. I lead my daughter along a ditch bank during a visit from Denver to Albuquerque. At four, she knows nothing of acequias, pottery shards, shadow men, or peacocks, so I tell her what I know, tossing a twig into a current still pulling me home. She looks me in the eye, same green as mine, and throws in her own stick. It bobs, spins, rights itself, and glides around the bend.

CONFLUENCE

My mother will not call my son by name. For months, she refers to him "baby," or "boy," not Cruz. She thinks my wife and I have marked him for suffering by naming him "cross."

One morning I phone her to explain what a priest from Mexico, a friend of my wife's, had said when we asked his opinion. Cruz, the priest said, means "tree of life." A beautiful name. In Mexico, Spain, Puerto Rico, and Peru, he explained, "Fiestas de la Cruz" are held in its honor.

My mother listens, then asks, "How's Junior?"

Ornery, I say through a sigh. Temperamental. The two of us are like night and day. Like my brother and I. Like my father and his brother. I lose my temper with my son as I never do with my daughter. Scold him when he pulls books from shelves. Swat his bottom when he yanks lamp cords. With him I'm different. Someone I don't recognize. I worry, I tell my mother, that I don't know how to be his father.

She pauses before answering. She was wrong about the name, she says, her voice a whisper. Cruz will not be the one to suffer. I will bear the burden.

❋

I can't sleep. Can't rest. The air is thick, muggy. I roll onto my side and check the clock: 2:17 a.m.

Slipping out of bed, I pad into the kitchen for a glass of water, peek into my children's room at my daughter and son, slide back beneath the sheets.

Crickets chirp. The curtains swell with the breeze.

The birthdays, I tell myself. He missed the birthdays. My father, the VA hospital report said, had struck his head somehow in the first weeks of June 1964. By mid-month, he couldn't speak clearly. By early July, he entered the hospital, never to leave.

My brother and two older sisters celebrate birthdays in mid-June and early July. Birthdays have always been special in my family. Our mother baked our favorite cakes, strung balloons, taped our snapshots to the front door. But the birthdays of 1964 must have been very different.

I picture my family on June 17 around the dining room table on the evening my oldest sister turned six. My mother bakes a devil's food cake, my sister's favorite, stacks a bright pyramid of gifts, lights birthday candles, leads us kids in song. I sit in my high chair, giddy from ice cream.

My father sits at the head of the table, mesmerized by the flickering flames. He blinks when my oldest sister kisses his cheek. Winces when my brother blasts a party horn. It is then, perhaps, that my mother notices his slurred speech, ends the party early, guides him to bed.

Three days later the scene is replayed. More balloons. A strawberry cake for my middle sister. This time, my father can't eat. Can't stay awake. The noise is painful.

The next morning, he enters the hospital.

On July 2, surgeons discuss the tumor in his brain, the cancer in his right lung, the strain upon his failing heart. The decision is unanimous: they cannot save him.

My brother turns six. His party is more subdued. Fewer balloons. Fewer gifts. My mother forces herself to sing. At the table, my father's chair stands empty.

❋

I swat my son harder than I intend. He snatches a red magic marker, uncaps it with his baby teeth, and proceeds to scribble on the white walls of our hallway.

He screams. Throws the pen in my face.

"What's wrong with you?" my wife says, hurrying after our wailing son. "You're so impatient. So . . . angry."

Alone in the backyard, I uncurl the garden hose and blast a stream of water at our row of spindly aspens.

My wife is right, I say to myself. I am angry. But not at my son.

My father was a pharmacist, a man of medicine. He should have known he was dying. He suffered a disabling heart attack in World War II, the report said. Took nitroglycerin tablets twice daily. Six months before his final hospitalization, he coughed blood. Still, with five young kids, he continued to smoke.

He should have known.

Or maybe my father, like most men of his generation, didn't know smoking was killing him. Maybe he thought he could stop any time. That he'd live to a hundred.

Or maybe he did know he was dying. Maybe he tried to prepare my family. Maybe that's why, before he entered the hospital, he sold the drugstore and applied for the disability pension, as my mother says.

Or maybe, I think, rolling up the hose so I can apologize to my son, when death came, it took him by surprise.

He'd fallen, the report said. He'd slipped on a shoelace, tripped on a porch step, or lost his balance reaching for a water glass. Coins spilled from his pockets. Keys clattered on the hardwood. Wallet photos slipped free. Pieces of my father slid under the davenport, behind the shelf, into the dark grate of the floor furnace.

❋

I find a river—the Y intersection of two shallow waterways, the Platte and Cherry Creek, among the high-rise lofts, brick warehouses, train tracks, and graffiti walls of downtown Denver. Confluence Park, it's called, an ancient Arapaho campground, a frontier-era gold-panning site, the birthplace of the city. At the water's edge, among the cycling paths, white Starbucks cups, urban pigeons, and homeless men, I notice flashes of my New Mexico home—cottonwoods, Russian olives, chamisal, and wild sunflowers—taking root amid the concrete and exhaust fumes.

I invite my son and daughter to join me. On Sunday mornings, I lead them across a narrow steel footbridge to the blond sand of the riverbank. I untie their sneakers, roll up their blue jeans, pat their behinds, and release them to play. My daughter sprinkles sand in the breeze like pixie dust. My son hurls stones into the rapids like hand grenades. I watch them giggle and jump, their heads ringed with silvery mist.

❋

My son and I walk alone through Confluence Park. At the water's edge, he drops my hand, forgoing pebble tossing to follow a path along Cherry Creek we've never taken.

"This way," he says. "I want to go this way."

Stifling an impulse to rein him in, I let him run, his wide little sandals slapping the hot concrete.

All morning he leads me deeper into the underbelly of downtown, pausing every few steps to point a chubby finger at a spiderweb sparkling with dew, a bumblebee collecting pollen from a clump of dandelions, or the golden flash of a minnow holding firm against the shallow green current—tiny miracles I would have otherwise overlooked.

After two hours he is too tired to walk, so I hoist him onto my shoulder. Within minutes he sleeps, his long red-brown curls dripping with perspiration. All the way home, his feet thump against my chest.

❋

Cruz has begun collecting rocks. He fills his pockets at the playground, then arranges his discoveries in neat rows along our dining room table.

"They're my friends," he says, brown eyes smiling.

One afternoon, he follows me to my backyard studio while I assemble relics for my father's descanso. He watches, frowning, as I place a cholla root beside a votive candle beside a nail beside a scattering of flint shards.

"What's that?" he asks, placing a finger on a bird-point I'd found with my mother in the Rio Puerco badlands.

"An arrowhead."

"An arrow?"

"No, silly. An arrowhead. The tip of an arrow."

Nodding, he hurries outside.

I rub the black stone between my fingers.

Arrowheads. Arrows.

My surname, Fletcher, means arrow-maker. Arrows represent swiftness, movement beyond set boundaries, knowledge, learning, and the sudden appearance of death. I often think about the men in my father's family and the restlessness that drove them, that drives me. I look at my own son now and the distance between us and wonder if I'm passing this legacy onto him, or if it will end here, with us, as I hope.

He toddles in with a gray pebble.

"Here, Dad. An arrow."

He holds it out until I take it, then watches, eyes alight, while I lay his offering beside the others.

WREATH

I

Weeds grow thick in my Denver garden, feeding on fertilizer and loam. Once, my wife and I scattered seeds from our homes in New Mexico, but season after season, this ground offers thorns. I pull with both hands, chop with a hoe, and rake my fingers through dry black soil.

Eyes closed, I feel for roots.

II

Late autumn. The sky a turquoise stone. My young mother watches her grandmother climb the steps of the rancho cellar.

"Come here, mí hijita." The old woman clutches a flour sack of shriveled bulbs packed in straw. "Carry these to the south wall. To plant them."

My mother, as always, does as she's told. She places the tubers in a shallow trench beneath the sala window, frowning down at the potato-like perennials.

"They're irises," her abuela says, watching her expression. "They'll like it here. Where it's warm."

"How can those ugly things be flowers? They look dead."

The old woman smiles.

"Patience," she says, and covers the bulbs with dirt.

III

The road to the ranch house is lined with wild sunflowers. My child mother reaches out the pickup window to brush their heart-shaped leaves. Her grandfather grins from behind the wheel, his face as brown as river clay.

Some farmers call them weeds, he says. Others cut them down. But blossoms attract bees. Bees make honey. And he knows where to find the secret hives along the Rio Grande.

My mother rubs her palms in the truck cab, dusting herself with pollen.

IV

Dusk settles over the valley in a lavender veil. My mother and her grandmother stand before the east wall of the ranch house, squinting at a row of shrubs swollen with buds.

"Look," the old woman whispers. "It's happening."

One by one the four-o'clocks unfold, cautious as butterflies, into trumpets of pink, yellow, purple, and red.

My mother wrinkles her nose. "How can they do that? In the dark?"

"It's a miracle," her grandmother says. "I wanted you to see it. To remember."

My mother cups a tiny blossom. Black seeds drip through her fingers.

V

Years before he meets my mother, my father, in middle age, experiments with hybrids. Alone in his Albuquerque garage after the deaths of his second wife, his siblings, and his parents, he grafts broken stems, empties dried pods, mixes soils, squeezes eyedroppers of clear salty liquid. In the pale blue halo of his growth lamp, he stares into his pots.

VI

My parents have five children in their seven years together. To commemorate our births, my mother plants roses on the north side of our home, a different blossom for each child. Scarlet climbers for my hotheaded older brother. Maroon Don Juans for my brooding big sister. Yellow fairies for my flighty middle sister. Golden darlings for my long-lashed baby sister. For me, she again chooses climbers, but coral, the color of dawn, of dusk.

VII

As a boy I stare into my father's face, into a photo that fits in my palm. He leans against the wall of a clapboard home I have never seen, young and strong, shoulders broad, work shirt rolled to his elbows. Here, he has no cigarette.

In his left hand he holds a pale feathery blossom. In his right, dark petals unfurl like smoke.

Dahlias, my mother says. From his family garden in Des Moines.

In life I know they must be yellow, pink, and purple, but here, in my eyes, they are black and white and shades of gray.

VIII

Outside my bedroom window, vines curl up the chain-link fence. Knotted. Twisted. Tight as my chest.

"Sleep," my mother says. "They're morning glories."

I dream of Jack-in-the-Beanstalk spirals and reaching clinging fingers. Come sunrise, violet trumpets, and silver diamonds filled with light.

IX

For my mother's fortieth birthday I make a special gift. I select from her back porch of ranch relics a square pine board. Alone in my room with my wood-burning iron set on high, I etch the round candle-flame face of a wild sunflower. For my mother, a blossom that will not fade.

X

My grandmother watches me through narrow eyes.

"He moves like Mr. Fletcher," she says in Spanish. "Like his father."

Squaring my shoulders, I glance up from my toy knights.

My mother kisses my cheek.

Later, in the mirror, I trace the lipstick rose.

XI

Beneath my daughter's Denver window a flower opens in a sidewalk crack. Wild, brought by the wind, it is a pinwheel of yellow, coral, lavender, violet. She bends to cup its face.

"Look, Daddy. An angel."

All summer, through broken stone, it blooms.

IN THE AMERICAN LIVES SERIES

Fault Line
by Laurie Alberts

Pieces from Life's Crazy Quilt
by Marvin V. Arnett

Songs from the Black Chair
A Memoir of Mental Illness
by Charles Barber

This Is Not the Ivy League
A Memoir
by Mary Clearman Blew

Driving with Dvořák
Essays on Memory and Identity
by Fleda Brown

Searching for Tamsen Donner
by Gabrielle Burton

American Lives
A Reader
edited by Alicia Christensen
introduced by Tobias Wolff

Out of Joint
A Private & Public Story
of Arthritis
by Mary Felstiner

Descanso for My Father
Fragments of a Life
Harrison Candelaria Fletcher

Falling Room
by Eli Hastings

Opa Nobody
by Sonya Huber

Hannah and the Mountain
Notes toward a Wilderness
Fatherhood
by Jonathan Johnson

Local Wonders
Seasons in the Bohemian Alps
by Ted Kooser

Bigger than Life
A Murder, a Memoir
by Dinah Lenney

What Becomes You
by Aaron Raz Link and Hilda Raz

Such a Life
by Lee Martin

Turning Bones
by Lee Martin

In Rooms of Memory
Essays
by Hilary Masters

Between Panic and Desire
by Dinty W. Moore

Sleep in Me
by Jon Pineda

Thoughts from a Queen-Sized Bed
by Mimi Schwartz

My Ruby Slippers
Finding Place on the Road
Back to Kansas
by Tracy Seeley

The Fortune Teller's Kiss
by Brenda Serotte

Gang of One
Memoirs of a Red Guard
by Fan Shen

Just Breathe Normally
by Peggy Shumaker

Scraping By in the Big Eighties
by Natalia Rachel Singer

In the Shadow of Memory
by Floyd Skloot

Secret Frequencies
A New York Education
by John Skoyles

Phantom Limb
by Janet Sternburg

Yellowstone Autumn
A Season of Discovery
in a Wondrous Land
by W. D. Wetherell

To order or obtain more information on these or other University of Nebraska Press titles, visit www.nebraskapress.unl.edu.